nosh4students

a fun cookbook

for students

by

D1016753

Joy May

Also by this author:

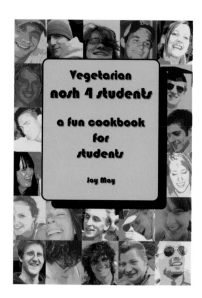

Published by:
inTRADE (GB) Ltd, 24 Beverley Crescent, Bedford, MK40 4BY. UK
Contact: joymay@mac.com

1st print 2002
2nd print 2004
3rd and 4th print 2005
Revised edition 2006
5th and 6th Print 2007
7th Print 2008

Author: Joy May

ISBN 0-9543179-3-9

Printed in Thailand

Introduction

This recipe book was inspired by my son Ben. He left for University with virtually no ability to cook, apart from toasted ham sandwiches. He did, however, like to eat. He soon began to ring home to ask how to cook various things. I sent him a few index cards with recipes on them, but they had no visual imagery to inspire him or for him to understand what the food should look like when finished. I searched for a good visual student cook book, but could not find one, so I decided to produce one, not just for Ben but for other students like him. I hope that you enjoy these recipes.

The stars * * * * * are an indication of how easy the recipes are. One star is very quick and easy, the five stars are for you to try when you are a little more accomplished. Most of the recipes in the book are healthy and well balanced, but there is the odd, over indulgent one!

Over half the recipes are either vegetarian or have a vegetarian alternative. If you are a 'fish eating vegetarian', then there are plenty of recipes for you to use.

The recipes are planned so that you need the minimum of pans, dishes and utensils and NO WEIGHING SCALES. A list of cooking equipment to take with you to University is on page 5.

Dedicated to Ben.
Thanks to Tim and Ron.

Author
Joy May

Contents

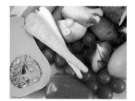

Introduction &
General Information 1 - 3

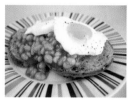

Basics 5 - 23

Limited Utensils

These recipes have been written
so that you will be able to produce them
using just the following utensils

To measure:
mug (approx ½ pint)
tablespoon, size mum serves with,
dessertspoon, one you eat cereal with,
teaspoon

To prepare and cook with:
wooden spoon
chopping board
sharp knife
small pan with lid
medium sized pan with lid
slotted turner (fish slice)
frying pan
casserole dish with lid
colander
flat roasting dish or metal non stick cooking tray
microwaveable plate
cheese grater

Golden Rules

Here are some things that will help you enjoy cooking and hopefully minimise discouraging failures.

1. Cooking should be FUN.

2. Plan ahead. If you can shop for your food for the week that is best. At the back of the book you will find sample menus for a week. Once you are used to using these, you can make your own menus and shopping lists. This means that you will not start a recipe and then find you do not have all the ingredients.

3. If you are a beginner, start by cooking the things you know you like first.

4. Read the recipe through before you begin, this helps to give an overall idea of what should be happening.

5. Get everything prepared first. For instance, don't try to chop vegetables whilst you are frying other things, especially if you are new to cooking.

6. If you have a house mate who can cook well, learn from them and get them to help you.

7. Don't try something new when you are cooking for others, rather do something you feel confident about.

8. If you are pushed for time, choose the simple recipes, one or two stars.

9. Don't have the heat source too high, either in the oven or on the top of the cooker.

10. Don't wander off whilst you are cooking things on the top of the cooker. Switch off the heat under pans if you go to answer the phone. It is easy to talk for a long time without realising it.

11. Try to make sure that your cooking area, your section of the fridge etc., are kept clean.

12. Try not to use out of date food, see 'How long can I keep this before it kills me', page 9.

Good buying ideas

1. Look through the recipe book before you go to the supermarket and buy ingredients for specific recipes, this way you will not waste food or be frustrated that you don't have all the ingredients to complete a recipe. See pages 131 - 133 for sample menus and shopping lists.

2. Buy in 'bulk' when things are on offer in the supermarkets and store excess in your freezer drawer.

3. If you have access to a freezer or part of a freezer, buy things like larger packets of frozen mince, chicken breasts or small chicken breast fillets, cubed meats, and fish fillets. This means that you will buy more than you need for one occasion, but it will cost much less in the long term.

4. Buy whole chickens and cook them, use the meat for one meal and then freeze the rest in portions. Use it later for sandwiches, baked potatoes, salads, risottos. Much cheaper than buying ready cooked chicken.

5. Keep things in stock like pasta, rice, flour, cornflour, salt and pepper.

6. Basic things to liven-up boring food are: Worcestershire sauce, soy sauce, a few freeze-dried herbs (basil, parsley, mixed herbs), stock cubes, pilau rice cubes or pilau rice seasoning, tomato sauce, tomato puree, and garlic.

7. Curry paste - much better than curry powder, use it in all sorts of things; liven up baked beans for instance!

8. Spare loaf of bread and pint of milk in the freezer, don't freeze milk in glass bottles, use the plastic bottles or cartons.

9. Always make sure that when you visit home you return to Uni having creamed off any excess from mum's cupboards!

What do I do if ??????

I don't have a microwave – To reheat a plate of food cover the plate with a pan lid or some foil. Place over a pan of boiling water and cook for 10 - 15 minutes. To defrost food – Wait!! Do not try to speed things up by placing the food in boiling water, especially things like chicken. Free flow, frozen mince is fine to use in many of the recipes in this book: just add it straight from the packet and put the rest of the pack back in the freezer.

I don't have a lid for the casserole – use some foil, tear off enough to wrap around the edges of the dish and mould it to the dish with your hands.

I don't have a pastry brush – use your fingers or a spoon.

I don't have a garlic press – peel the garlic and put on a board. Put a chopping knife flat on the garlic and the heel of your hand on top, press down hard and squash the garlic, then chop the garlic finely.

Everything I cook in the oven is burnt! – It could be that if you have an older oven the thermostat is not working quite as well as it should. Don't give up, just adjust by lowering the temperature you set it to.

Everything I cook in the oven is undercooked! – Oven temperatures vary, check whether you have a Centigrade or Fahrenheit oven, then check the temperature on the recipe. If you have followed the instructions correctly it could be that your oven thermostat is old, so increase the temperature slightly.

If everything you cook on top of the cooker is burnt – either you need to keep the heat turned down or you just need to keep an eye on things. You can't go off and ring your mates whilst trying to cook successfully.

All the oven temperatures in the book are based on having a Centigrade fan oven. Here is a chart to help you adjust the temperatures if you do not have a fan or Centigrade oven.

Gas	C	Fan C	F	Oven Temperature
¼	110	90	225	Very cool
½	120	100	250	Very cool
1	140	120	275	Cool or slow
2	150	130	300	Cool or slow
3	160	140	325	Warm
4	180	160	350	Moderate
5	190	170	375	Moderately hot
6	200	180	400	Fairly hot
7	220	200	425	Hot
8	230	210	450	Very hot
9	240	220	475	Very hot

Basics

How long can I keep this before it kills me?

Raw meat – I day in the fridge. Bacon – 2 to 3 days in the fridge

Cooked meat – 3 days maximum in the fridge

Eggs – 2 to 3 weeks

Milk – 2 days once opened. Unopened it should keep until the 'best before' date, but needs to be in the fridge.

Butter and margarine spreads – 2 to 3 weeks

Cheese – I week once opened, 2 weeks unopened, keep cheese wrapped with cling film or it will go dry and horrid. Green mould on cheese, other than the blue varieties, means that it is best thrown away.

Vegetables – vary, some keep better in the fridge, others out.

Onions and potatoes – keep for about one week, best out of the fridge and in a dark place. Once potatoes have gone green, they are not very good for you!

Green vegetables – keep better in the fridge as do carrots, parsnips etc.

Salad, lettuce, cucumber, tomatoes, peppers etc. – keep in the fridge up to a week. Keep lettuce covered.

Keep everything covered in the fridge, this helps things keep better and rules out cross contamination if you share a fridge with someone who leaves disgusting things in there! Cling film is a wonderful and inexpensive invention.

Don't keep tins in the fridge: once opened the tin will begin to make the food taste of metal and not do you much good.

Basic Hygiene in the Kitchen

Keep your dishcloth and tea towels clean!

Clean your chopping board after cutting raw meat!

Wash up now and then!!???!

Take care when reheating food that you heat it thoroughly.

9

Vegetables

Depending on your taste, you do not always need to peel veggies. Washing them is a good idea. Larger things like potatoes and carrots need to be cut into pieces before cooking, broccoli broken into 'small trees' and so on.

Boiled vegetables Generally most vegetables need to be cooked in just enough water to cover them. Bring the water to the boil. Once boiling, add the vegetables and a little salt and simmer gently with the lid on the pan. If you keep the source of the heat low, not only will you preserve a little more nutrition in the vegetables, but you will also avoid burnt pans and very mucky cookers where the pans have boiled over.

Here are some approximate cooking times

Swedes and Turnips	20 - 25 minutes
Potatoes, parsnips, carrots	10 - 15 minutes
Cauliflower	10 minutes
Broccoli	5 minutes, boiling gently.
Green beans	5 - 10 minutes
Spinach	1 - 2 minutes, just enough to make the leaves wilt. You will only need a little water in the bottom of the pan.
Leeks	5 - 10 minutes
Cabbage	5 - 10 minutes. Again, you only need a little water, drain after cooking and add some butter and black pepper. Return to the pan and cook for another 2 minutes to dry the cabbage a little.
Sugar Snaps	2 minutes, Mange Tout - 1 minute

If you really want the fuss of **mashed potatoes,** it is best to peel them first. Boil them as above: once they are cooked through, mash them, either with a fork or a potato masher, whilst adding a little milk and butter.

Jacket Potatoes see page 15.

Roast vegetables. Preheat the oven to 180°C/gas mark 6. Cut the vegetables into medium sized, fairly even pieces. Put them on a flat roasting/baking tray and sprinkle them with salt and olive oil. Turn them over with your hands to make sure that the oil is covering all the pieces. Set them back on the tray with flat sides up. If the flat sides are on the tray itself they will tend to stick. Sprinkle with rosemary if you wish. Put in the middle of the oven for 30 minutes. Check to see if any are getting too brown; maybe the ones around the edge. Move, or turn over as necessary. Put back in the oven for another 30 minutes. If you want to roast peppers, rub them with oil, place on a baking tray and cook for 25 minutes.

Things to roast - potatoes (cut into 2 or 3 pieces), butternut squash (cut into 2" chunks), parsnips (cut into 4, lengthways), sweet potatoes (cut into 2 or 3 pieces), onions (cut into 6 wedges), fennel (cut into 4 wedges). If you want to roast tomatoes; cut the skin, rub with a little oil, and add to the tray about 15 minutes before the end of the cooking time.

Roast vegetables are great with things like sausages, chicken drumsticks, beefburgers etc.

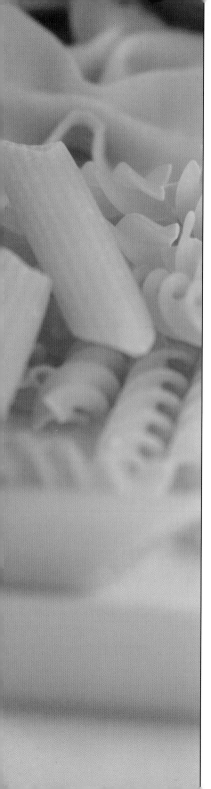

How to cook pasta

There are innumerable kinds of pasta to choose from in the shops, made from different ingredients. Most will have instructions on the packets as to how to cook them. Just in case you have lost the packet, here are some general guidelines:

I. Spaghetti

For one person, depending on appetite, you need a bunch of spaghetti approximately the diameter of a 50p piece. Boil sufficient water in a pan to cover the spaghetti whilst cooking. Once the water is boiling, lower the spaghetti sticks into the water. Once the half that is in the water has softened slightly, push the other half in. Take care not to get your fingers in the water. Simmer for 8 - 10 minutes. Test one piece to see if it is cooked. Drain the water off and add one teaspoon of butter or olive oil, mix around and this will stop the spaghetti sticking together.

2. Most other pastas

Again, boil enough water to cover the pasta. Once the water is boiling, add the pasta. One mug of dried pasta is plenty for one person with a very healthy appetite. Simmer for the appropriate time, drain and add butter or olive oil to prevent the pasta sticking together.

3. Cooking times

Tagliatelle, smaller pasta twists, small macaroni takes approx. 5 minutes.

Riccioli, Tirali, Fusilli and thicker twists 8 - 11 minutes.

Some varieties of pasta, like penne, may take as long as 15 minutes to cook.

Pasta is better slightly undercooked than overcooked.

How to cook rice

There are many different types of rice to buy. I would recommend that you use basmati. It is slightly more expensive than long grain or quick cook rice, but has a much better flavour and texture than the cheaper varieties.

Rice for one person = ½ mug rice + 1 mug water. Knorr Pilau cube (or other rice flavour cubes) or 1 teaspoon of pilau rice flavouring transform rice from tasteless to yummy.

1. Using a pan with a lid, bring the water to the boil, add the flavour cube and stir until it has dissolved.
2. Add the rice and stir, bring back to the boil. Once boiling turn down the heat to very low so that the rice simmers gently. Put the lid on the pan and cook for approximately 15 minutes. Do not stir whilst the rice is cooking or you will make it sticky. The rice should be cooked once the water has disappeared. Don't keep lifting the lid, as during the last part of the cooking time the rice is steaming.
3. Test the rice after the 15 minutes. If the rice is still too crunchy and the water has all gone, then you have boiled it too quickly. Add a little more water, replace the lid and cook for another 5 minutes.

To make egg fried rice

1. Cook the rice as above using a pilau rice cube.
2. Using one egg per quantity of rice, beat the egg in a mug. Heat some butter or oil in a frying pan. Pour the egg into the pan and allow it to spread all over the base. Cook until the egg is set, remove from the pan and cut the egg up into strips.
3. Using the same frying pan add a little more oil and some finely chopped onion (¼ an onion per person), fry until the onion is browned.
4. If the frying pan is large enough for the quantity of rice you have cooked, add the rice and egg to the onions and stir well. If you have a larger quantity, then add the onions and the egg to the rice pan.

'Cook in Sauces'

There are many 'cook in sauces' on the market and they are very easy to use, but are, of course, much more expensive than making sauces from basic ingredients. It is good to get mum to buy you a few when you come back to Uni, they make life easier. Save them for when you are really pressed for time and need a good meal. Here are some ideas to help you to use them.

Most 'economy meats', **i.e. chicken thighs and legs, stewing meats etc.** need to cook for a long time if they are to be edible. You can cook them in the sauces, but you will need to add extra liquid as the sauces will dry up during the cooking time. Add the 'cook in sauce' to the chicken thighs, for example, but add another ½ jar of water, mix well and cook in a covered dish in the oven for 1 ½ hours with the heat at 170°C/gas reg 5. It is best to take the skins off chicken thighs as they contain a lot of fat and will make the dish very greasy if they are not removed. Stewing meats, lamb or beef will take the same length of time to cook. Chicken legs will cook at the same temperature, but only need 45 minutes to 1 hour to cook, depending on how tender you like them.

If you are using **chicken breasts or small chicken breast fillets,** cut the meat into bite-size chunks and fry in a little oil or butter for approximately 4 - 5 minutes. Once the meat is cooked through, add the 'cook in sauce' and once boiling, simmer for a further 2 - 3 minutes.

If you are using **mince,** fry in a little oil. Once the mince is no longer pink, add the 'cook in sauce', bring to the boil and then simmer for 2 - 3 minutes.

If you are using a **Bolognese Sauce,** fry the mince in a little oil first and then add the sauce. You can eat this with spaghetti or pasta. Alternatively you can add to dry pasta, stir together, put in a casserole dish, sprinkle with grated cheese and bake in the oven for 20 - 25 minutes 180°C/gas reg 6.

If you have **left-over cooked meat,** for example, if you have cooked a chicken, simply add to the sauce and bring to the boil, simmer for 4 - 5 minutes to make sure that the meat is properly reheated.

If all you have left in your freezer or fridge are **sausages,** you can use these with 'cook in sauces', brown them well and make sure they are cooked through, cut into bite-size pieces and add the sauce.

If you want to eat **vegetarian** food, add a 'cook in sauce' to uncooked pasta and cook in the oven, uncovered, for 20 - 25 minutes, 180°C/gas reg 6. If you are using a Bolognese type sauce, grate some cheese on the top, this will add extra flavour. **Vegetarians** can use 'cook in sauces' with cooked vegetables. Follow the instructions for Vegetable Bake on page 83. Adding the sauce to raw vegetables will not work well.

Jacket potatoes

1. Use medium or large potatoes. Always slit the skin with a knife before baking or it may explode in the oven or the microwave.
2. Bake in the oven, 200°C/gas reg 7, for 1 hour. If you are short of time, cook in the microwave on full power for 5 minutes and then in the oven for 30 minutes. If you are really short of time, you can cook in the microwave for 7 - 10 minutes on full power. You will only get the crisp jackets if you cook the potato in the oven. Timing depends on how large the potato is.
3. When the potato is cooked, cut it open and add any of the following suggestions, together with a little butter to moisten:

Baked beans.
Cheese, grated.
Tuna and mayonnaise and sweetcorn.
Cottage cheese, on its own or with shrimps, tuna, ham, tomatoes, peppers etc.
Cooked chicken and mayonnaise. You can add a little mustard to the mayonnaise or ½ teaspoon curry paste.
Chilli con carne, recipe page 46 or you could buy a tin.
Smoked mackerel. Take the skin off and break up slightly, add some mayonnaise.
Crispy bacon and hard boiled eggs, chopped up together.
Natural Yogurt, pepper, sweetcorn, chilli powder.
Natural yogurt, sliced mushrooms, 1 teaspoon tomato puree, 1 teaspoon mild curry paste..

Jacket potatoes are good served with a little salad, lettuce, tomatoes, cucumber and spring onions.

Bread

Eggie Bread
1. Break an egg into a mug and beat with a fork. Pour out onto a plate.
2. Dip a thick slice of bread into the egg and let the bread soak up the egg on both sides.
3. Put 2 teaspoons of butter in a frying pan and heat until the butter starts to bubble. Add the bread and cook gently until both sides are browned.
4. Serve with beans and HP or tomato sauce.
5. You can make this sweet by adding a dessertspoon of sugar to the egg at the beginning.

Cinnamon Toast
1. Toast bread very lightly on both sides and butter on one side.
2. Make a mixture of 1 teaspoon cinnamon and 3 teaspoon sugar and sprinkle on top of the toast.
3. Put it back under the grill and heat until the sugar has dissolved.
4. Americans eat this with boiled eggs for breakfast. Brits eat it as a snack.

Bread and butter pudding
If you have a large amount of bread left over, slice and butter it, arrange it in a casserole dish, sprinkle with 3 - 4 dessertspoons of sugar. You can add currants and/or sprinkle on a teaspoon of cinnamon if you have it. Beat 2 or 3 eggs in a bowl and add a mug of milk, pour over the bread. Place in the oven at 180°C/gas reg 6 for 30 - 35 mins, the top should be browned.

French Toast
Butter the bread before toasting. Toast the butter side first and then the reverse side.

Garlic Bread
This works best with bread sticks, but you can do the same with other breads; for example, buns.
1. Take 2 large cloves of garlic, peel and crush them, mix well with 2 tablespoons butter. You can add 1 teaspoon of freeze dried chives or parsley, if you wish.
2. Make diagonal cuts in the bread stick, ensuring that you don't cut right through. Push the butter into the cuts.
3. Wrap the bread stick in foil and place on a baking sheet or oven-proof dish. Cook for 6 - 7 minutes at 200°C/gas reg 7.

Fried bread
Heat some oil or butter in a frying pan, dip both sides of the bread in the oil to absorb it evenly, then fry on both sides for 2 minutes until browned.

Stuff on toast

This may seem very obvious, but here are a few ideas to make your 'stuff on toast' a bit tastier!

Ideas

Beans on toast with egg on top, great with HP sauce. Toast the bread, heat the beans and then fry or poach the eggs, see page 20.
Cheese on toast -   first, very lightly toast the bread, as you will return it to the grill to cook the cheese. Butter the toast. At this stage you can add things under the cheese such as pickle, marmite or sliced tomatoes. Slice or grate the cheese and place on top. Make sure the cheese covers the edges of the toast, it will protect the corners of the bread from being burned. Use a slotted turner to put the toast back under the grill. Watch the grill as it will cook quite quickly. If you are just putting cheese on, you can sprinkle Worcestershire sauce on it. You can use the cheese sauce recipe from page 23, add a pinch of paprika to spice it up, and just pour over the toast.
Scrambled egg, with or without cheese, see page 20.
Cream Cheese with cucumber or tomatoes
There are a number of toasty toppers you can buy in the supermarket.
The obvious things are jams etc, but chocolate spread, peanut butter, honey make good comfort food!
You can use toast as a pizza base following the instructions for mini pizzas on page 61, just substitute a little tomato sauce for the 'basic tomato sauce'.

Pitta bread fillings

Pitta breads make a tasty alternative to sandwiches, they are inexpensive and readily available in the supermarkets. You can generally get more filling in them than in a sandwich! You can put almost anything in, but here are a few suggestions. Iceberg lettuce works well because it is a crispy contrast to the pitta bread.

Ham, mayo, lettuce, spring onions, cucumber, tomato
Tuna, sweetcorn, lettuce, mayo, spring onions and cucumber
Fetta cheese, with lettuce, tomato, cucumber and mayo
Cooked chicken with salad and mayo
Beef with mustard and salad
Cooked sausages, sliced with mayo and salad
Bacon lettuce and tomato
Cottage Cheese, iceberg lettuce, tomatoes, onion rings and cucumber

Basics

Sandwiches

Ideas for fillings
~ Bacon (plus brown sauce).
~ Bacon (cooked hot and crisp) and banana (not cooked), go on give it a try!
~ Honey and banana.
~ Scrambled eggs (can add some cheese to egg whilst cooking, see page 20).
~ Cottage cheese or cream cheese, both great with jam or honey and bananas.
~ Cottage cheese with tomatoes or cucumber, remember to season well.
~ Cream cheese with tomato and ham.
~ Egg mayonnaise - hard boiled eggs, chopped and mixed with mayo, season well.
~ Salmon and cucumber - can add mayonnaise.
~ Tuna, hard boiled egg, spring onion and mayonnaise.
~ Cheese and tomato.
~ Ham, cheese, lettuce and mayo.   ~ Fried egg.
~ Cheese and pickle.   ~ Marmite!
~ Cheese and jam, raspberry works well.   ~ Peanut butter and jam or marmalade.
~ Boiled egg and tomato.   ~ Peanut butter and honey and/or bananas.
~ Bacon and mayonnaise.   ~ Chicken and mayonnaise with lettuce.
~ Sausages and brown sauce.   ~ Bacon, lettuce and tomato.

Toasted sandwiches
Your mum may have an old sandwich toaster up in the loft or out in the garage. Seek it out and take it with you to Uni. The idea of the sandwich toaster was to make the sandwich with the butter side of the bread on the outside, this makes the bread more tasty on the toasted side. If you make toasted sandwiches under the grill, put the buttered side on the inside or the butter will just melt and drip off. You can use all the above fillings in toasted sandwiches, apart from the ones containing lettuce or cucumber.

Eggs

Poach

1. Using a small pan or frying pan, half fill with water and add a good pinch of salt. Bring to the boil, then turn down until the water is only just moving.
2. Break the egg into a mug or cup, gently pour into the water. Do not stir or turn the heat up, just let it cook gently. It will take 2 - 4 minutes, depending on the size of the egg.
3. Once the egg has gone opaque, gently lift out with a slotted turner and let the water drain from it.
4. Great with beans on toast, tomato sauce or HP.

Scramble

1. Using a small milk pan, preferably non stick, add 2 teaspoons butter, heat gently until the butter bubbles.
2. Break the egg into the pan and add salt and pepper. Stir slowly, breaking up the egg yolk.
3. When the egg is almost set, take off the heat. The egg will continue to cook in its own heat. If you cook it too long it will become rubbery.
4. You can add grated cheese and/or chopped tomatoes half-way through the cooking.

Fry

Not the healthiest way to eat eggs, but if you must, here is how to do it. (They make a great supper snack as fried egg butties.)

1. Heat 2 teaspoons butter in the frying pan until the butter just bubbles.
2. Break the egg into a mug and then gently pour into the frying pan.
3. Cook on medium heat until the egg is set.
4. Using a slotted turner, turn the egg over half-way through cooking if you want 'easy over' hard yolk.

Boil

1. Using a small pan fill ⅔ full with water and bring to the boil.
2. Lower the egg into the pan on a spoon.
3. Simmer briskly for 3 minutes for a very runny egg, 5 minutes and you will still be able to dip your soldiers in the runny yolk, 12 minutes and it will be hard-boiled.

Omelettes

Instructions for a basic omelette for 1 person

1. Put two or three eggs in a mug and beat well with a fork, add two tablespoons of water.
2. Switch on the grill to full heat to warm up.
3. Melt about a dessertspoon of butter in the frying pan. Once it begins to 'bubble' pour the egg mixture into the pan.
4. As it sets on the bottom of the pan, gently move the set egg with fish slice and allow the runny egg to take its place. Do this with two or three sweeping movements, don't stir or you will get scrambled egg. Repeat this process once more.
5. While there is still a little runny egg on the top, add whatever filling you want, top with cheese (not essential) and place the frying pan under the hot grill. Watch carefully, the omelette should rise. Once it is browned on the top, remove from the grill and turn out onto a plate. Serve with salad, garlic bread or baked potatoes.

Suggested fillings - cheese, tomato, mushrooms, fried onions, crispy grilled bacon cut into pieces, cooked chicken, ham or any combination of these ingredients.

Sweet omelettes - add fruit (strawberries, raspberries or blackcurrants are the best kind of fruit), sugar, cinnamon or jam.

Pancakes ★ ★

Pancakes are easy to make and are good fun when you have friends around. Just make sure you are not the only one standing cooking them. Tossing them is always fun, catching them not guaranteed.

Recipe   Makes about 6.

2 eggs
6 tablespoons plain flour
milk
Trex or white Flora to fry (you can use oil but a lard type is best)

1. Beat the eggs and flour together in a bowl or jug, gradually add the milk, making sure there are no lumps. The mixture should be as thin as single cream, quite thin, but not as thin as milk.
2. Heat about ½" cube of lard in a frying pan. When the fat begins to smoke a little, pour approximately 2 tablespoons of the mixture into the pan, tip the pan around so that the mixture spreads over the surface of the pan. Let the mixture cook for about I minute.
3. Gently lift the edge of the pancake to see if it is browned. Once browned turn the pancake with a slotted turner or toss and then cook the other side.
4. Serve with lemon juice and sugar, undiluted squashes, any kind of ice cream, maple syrup, golden syrup, fruit such as strawberries, jam or ice cream sauces.

You can make savoury pancakes. Use the same method as above, make fillings such as tuna and mayonnaise, cottage cheese and tomato, chicken and ham in a cheese sauce (see page 23).

Quick cheese sauce ⋆

For 1 serving
Preparation and cooking time 10 - 15 minutes

Vegetarian

This is a simple, useful and versatile basic sauce.

1 mug grated cheese	1 mug milk
1 tablespoon flour	⅛ teaspoon paprika
1 teaspoon butter	salt and pepper

1. Put the grated cheese into a saucepan, add the flour, salt, pepper and paprika and stir well.
2. Add the milk and butter, bring to the boil, stirring all the time, the sauce should thicken.

Double this quantity for vegetable bake, lasagna and cauliflower cheese.

Italian Soup ★

Serves 2 - 3
Preparation and cooking time 20 minutes

Vegetarian

The ingredients for this soup may seem a little complicated, don't worry if you don't have them all: the celery and the spinach can be left out if you wish.

1 small potato, diced	3 mugs water
1 carrot, diced	1 chicken stock cube, crumbled
1 onion, chopped	2 pieces frozen spinach
3 teaspoons butter	1 teaspoon freeze dried basil
½ red pepper, chopped	¼ cup small macaroni
1 - 2 celery sticks, sliced	1 tablespoon tomato puree
14 oz/400g tin of tomatoes	salt and pepper
2 cloves garlic, crushed	

1. Melt butter in saucepan, add onions, potato, carrot, pepper, celery and garlic and cook for two minutes, stirring well.
2. Add the tin of tomatoes, tomato puree, water and stock cube, bring to the boil. Cook for ten minutes, then add the macaroni and cook for a further four minutes.
3. Add the spinach and the basil and season well.

Vegetable Soup ⋆

Serves 1
Preparation and cooking time 20 minutes

Vegetarian

This is a good, easy soup for a winter day, the ingredients listed make a good combination, but you can use whatever vegetables you have to hand.

1 small potato, cut into cubes
1 medium sized carrot, peeled and sliced
1 stick of celery, cut into pieces
½ medium onion, chopped
pieces of ham (optional)
½ vegetable or chicken stock cube

1½ mugs water
¼ mug frozen peas
1 teaspoon butter
1 teaspoon flour
salt and pepper

1. Fry the onion in the butter.
2. Add the potatoes and carrots and cook for about 30 seconds.
3. Add flour and mix in with the vegetables already in the pan.
4. Add the water and stock cube and bring to the boil, simmer for 10 minutes or until the vegetables are cooked.
5. Add the celery and the peas, cook for 2 minutes.
6. Add the pieces of ham and cook for 1 minute.
7. Serve with bread.

Mulligatawny Soup ★

Serves 2 - 3
Preparation time 10 minutes, cooking time 20 minutes.

This is more of a stew than a soup, it is very substantial. If you reheat this soup the next day, make sure that it boils and then simmers slowly for about 3 - 4 minutes. Alternatively, reheat in a microwave for 2 minutes on a high setting.

1 teaspoon cooking oil
½ onion, chopped
1 carrot, peeled and sliced
1 stick celery, cut into small pieces
1 eating apple, cut into chunks
2 - 3 teaspoons curry paste (mild)
4 small chicken breast fillets (raw), cut into small pieces
salt and pepper

½ teaspoon ground coriander
3 mugs water
1 chicken stock cube
14 oz/400g tin of chopped tomatoes
¼ mug long grain rice

1. Fry the onion, carrot and celery.
2. Add the rest of the ingredients and bring to the boil. Simmer for 20 minutes, stirring occasionally.

Sausage Soup ★ ★

Serves 1   Preparation and cooking time 15 - 20 minutes

This soup is inexpensive, easy to cook, tasty and filling. Reheating sausages is never a good idea, so it is best to make only as much as you will eat at one time. You can always make more and share it.

4 small or 2 large sausages (spicy sausages work well with this recipe).
1 small onion, chopped
1 teaspoon butter
¼ mug pasta, (tagliatelle, macaroni, or small twists)

1 beef stock cube
1 x 7 oz/200g tin baked beans
salt and pepper
3 teaspoons Worcestershire sauce
1½ mugs water

1. Fry the onion in butter.
2. Add the water, stock cube and pasta, bring to the boil and simmer gently for 4 - 5 minutes.
3. While the pasta is simmering, cook the sausages. Fry or grill them.
4. Add the sausages, beans and Worcestershire sauce. Cook for 2 minutes. Season with salt and pepper.

Soups

Spicy Soup and Herby Dumplings ★ ★ ★

Serves 2
Preparation and cooking time approximately 30 minutes

Vegetarian

This is a meal for when you are cold and hungry, it's tasty and inexpensive. Keep some suet in the fridge as you can use it to make pie crusts, see recipe on page 37.

1 large carrot, peeled and sliced
1 large onion, chopped.
1 large potato, cut into pieces
14 oz/400g tin chopped tomatoes
1½ mugs water
1 beef or vegetable stock cube
2 teaspoons butter to fry
3 - 4 mushrooms, sliced
1 teaspoon curry paste, more if you like it hot.

Dumplings
Salt and pepper
1 teaspoon coriander leaves (freeze dried)
½ mug suet
1 mug self raising flour, plain won't work, the dumplings will be solid
1 egg + a little water to mix

1. Fry the onions in the butter, add potatoes and carrots, cook for 30 seconds.
2. Add the tin of tomatoes, stock cube, curry paste, water and mushrooms. Bring to the boil and leave to simmer gently while you make the dumplings.
3. In a bowl, a cereal bowl will do, mix together the flour, suet, salt, pepper and coriander.
4. In a mug, beat the egg and a little water, add to the flour mixture and stir around. Add just enough of the egg and water to form a soft ball of dough. Don't make it too wet, you may not need to use all the liquid.
5. Put some flour onto a board or plate and turn the mixture out onto it. Squeeze gently to form a ball, cut into 8 pieces, forming each one into a ball.
6. Add these to the simmering soup and cook gently for 10 - 15 minutes. If you have a lid, put it on the pan and the dumplings will cook quicker. Don't stir the soup too much or you will break up the dumplings.

Chicken and Sweetcorn Soup ★★

Serves 1
Preparation and cooking time 10 minutes

This soup is more substantial and nutritious than many take-away versions. It is just as tasty and will form a meal in itself.

1 teaspoon butter	1 teaspoon soy sauce
1 teaspoon cornflour	¼ tin sweetcorn
1 chicken stock cube	salt and pepper
1 mug water	1 teaspoon freeze dried chives
1 egg	

3 spring onions, chopped, you could use an ordinary onion.
2 small pieces uncooked chicken breast fillet, cut into small pieces

1. Fry the onions in the butter until soft.
2. Add the water, soy sauce and stock cube. Bring to the boil.
3. Add the chicken (you must use chicken breast or the meat will not cook properly) and sweetcorn, cook until the chicken is no longer pink, approximately 2 - 3 minutes.
4. Mix the cornflour with a little water in a mug. Add to the soup, stirring well until it comes back to the boil and thickens. Don't let the soup boil for a long time. Add the chives.
5. Beat the egg in a mug and pour into the soup. Leave until the egg begins to set and then stir once only, this way the egg will stay together.
6. Cook until the egg goes white. Add salt and pepper.

Pasta with Spicy Sausages ★★

Serves 2   Preparation time 20 minutes

Vegetarian option

You can use vegetarian sausages with this recipe and add ½ teaspoon chilli powder to the tomato sauce.

6 spicy sausages, pork, beef or vegetarian
I small onion, chopped
I clove garlic, chopped
I x 14 oz/400g tin chopped tomatoes
I tablespoon tomato puree
I teaspoon mixed herbs
I mug of penne pasta

1. Cook the pasta and drain well.
2. Fry or grill the sausages and then take them out of the pan. Cut them into bite size pieces.
3. Fry the onions and garlic for 3 - 4 minutes.
4. Add the tinned tomatoes and tomato puree to the pan and bring to the boil. Allow to simmer for 4 - 5 minutes for the flavours to blend.
5. Add the sausages, herbs and the pasta to the pan and cook for a further 2 - 3 minutes until everything is heated through.
6. Serve and enjoy.

Sausage with Apple and Mustard ★★

Serves 2   Preparation time 15 minutes, cooking time 10 - 15 minutes

This is a very simple 'all in one pot' meal to make. It is inexpensive and gives sausages a very different flavour, the apples, mustard and chutney give a sweet and savoury tang to the dish.

oil to fry
4 - 6 sausages, pork, herby or vegetarian
1 small onion, sliced
1 eating apple, cut into chunks
2 tablespoons of sweet chutney
1 stock cube, chicken, beef or vegetable
1 mug of boiling water
1 teaspoon of mustard
2 medium potatoes
salt and pepper

Vegetarian option

1. Wash the potatoes and cut into small cubes. It is not necessary to peel them.
2. Fry the sausages in the oil in a wok or frying pan until they are browned on all sides. Take them from the pan.
3. Fry the onions, and potatoes until they begin to brown.
4. Dissolve the stock cube in the mug of boiling water and add to the wok. Add the apples, mustard, chutney and return the sausages to the wok. Bring everything to the boil and then turn down the heat and simmer for 10 - 15 minutes until the potatoes are cooked. Stir a couple of times during the cooking process. Season well with salt and pepper and serve.

Sausages

Sausage and Bean Casserole★★

Serves 2   Preparation time 25 minutes

This dish is an easy, inexpensive and very nourishing one, especially in the winter. If you are sharing a house with others it's great to double the quantity and share it together. If you want to spice it up a little, add some curry paste.

4 large sausages, pork, beef or vegetarian
oil to fry
I small onion, chopped
I clove garlic, chopped finely
I small green pepper, cut into slices
I x 14 oz/400g tin of chopped tomatoes
I x 14 oz/400g tin baked beans
I tablespoon Worcestershire sauce
I tablespoon tomato puree
baked potatoes or rice to serve

Vegetarian option

1. Cook sausages under grill.
2. Using the oil, fry the onions and garlic in a wok if you have one, otherwise use a frying pan. Cook for 2 - 3 minutes and then add the peppers and cook for a further 5 minutes. Season well with salt and pepper.
3. Add the tinned tomatoes, tomato puree and the Worcestershire sauce. Cook for 5 - 6 minutes.
4. Cut the sausages and add to the pan along with the beans.
5. Serve with baked potatoes or rice.

Sausage Pie ★ ★ ★

Serves 2   Preparation time 15 minutes, cooking time 25 minutes

2 medium potatoes	1 vegetable stock cube
oil to fry	½ mug hot water
½ onion, chopped	½ mug grated cheese
1 leek, cut into 1cm slices	1 teaspoon butter
2 cloves garlic, finely chopped	salt and pepper
4 thick pork and herb or vegetarian sausages	1 teaspoon cornflour

Vegetarian option

1. Wash and dice the potatoes.   Boil for 10 minutes. Drain and return to the pan, add the teaspoon of butter and shake the potatoes in the pan to distribute the butter. Leave to one side.

2. Put oven on to heat 180°C/gas reg 6.

3. Cook the sausages in a little oil, using a frying pan. When the sausages are brown, remove from pan and cut into bite-size pieces.

4. Fry the onion and garlic for 2 - 3 minutes in the same pan you have taken the sausages from. Add the leek and cook for a further 2 - 3 minutes.

5. Put the vegetable stock cube in a mug and fill up to ½ with boiling water, mix the cube until it dissolves. Add to the other things in the frying pan and bring to the boil.

6. Blend the cornflour with a little cold water and then add to the frying pan, stirring quickly, the sauce should thicken. Season well with salt and pepper.

7. Add the sausages back to the pan and stir. Pour into a casserole dish. Pile the potatoes on the top and sprinkle over with grated cheese. Bake for 25 - 30 minutes until the cheese has browned.

Roast Potatoes and Sausages ⋆

Serves 2   Preparation time 5 minutes, cooking time 1 hour

Vegetarian option

Very quick and simple way to get delicious roast potatoes, an inexpensive taste of home.

6 - 8 sausages, beef, pork or vegetarian
4 - 6 potatoes
1 tablespoon cooking oil
1 onion
salt and pepper

1. Preheat the oven to 180°C/gas reg 6.
2. Wash potatoes and cut into large wedges, peel the onion and cut into 6.
3. Oil the casserole dish or baking tray and place the potatoes, sausages and onions in it. Brush everything with the oil (use your fingers if you do not have a brush) and season well with salt and pepper.
4. Put in the oven for 30 minutes. Take out of the oven and carefully turn things over so that they brown on the other side. Cook for a further 20 - 30 minutes or until everything is browned.
5. Serve with baked beans.

Sausages

Sausage and Egg Bake ★ ★

Serves 2   Preparation time 10 - 15 minutes, cooking time 15 - 20 minutes

1 onion, chopped finely
1 clove of garlic, chopped finely
6 herby, spicy or vegetarian sausages
1 x 14 oz/400g tin of cannelloni beans
1 x 14 oz/400g tin of chopped tomatoes
freeze dried basil
2 eggs
1 teaspoon of tomato puree

Vegetarian option

1. Preheat the oven to 180°C/gas reg 6. Grease a casserole dish.
2. Fry the sausages in a frying pan until browned. Remove from pan.
3. Fry the onion and garlic for 2 - 3 minutes, stirring frequently.
4. Add the tin of tomatoes and tomato puree, stir and bring to the boil. Cook for 2 - 3 minutes.
5. Rinse the beans and drain well. Add to the pan, continue to cook.
6. Cut each sausage into 4 and add to the pan, stir well and take off the heat. Add the basil and season well with salt and pepper.
7. Pour the mixture into the casserole dish. Break the 2 eggs over the top of the mixture.
8. Bake in the oven for 10 - 15 minutes until the eggs are cooked.
9. Serve with fresh, crusty bread or baked potatoes.

Burgers in Tomato Sauce ★ ★ ★

Serves 4   Preparation time 15 minutes, cooking time 35 minutes

Burgers
1 x 500g pack of minced beef
1 onion, finely chopped
1 egg, beaten
salt and pepper

Sauce
1 x 14 oz/400g tin of chopped tomatoes
1 teaspoon sugar
1 clove of garlic, finely chopped
1 teaspoon freeze dried basil
1 tablespoon tomato puree

1. Put the oven on to preheat at 200°C/gas reg 7. If you are serving this with jacket potatoes put them in the oven now.
2. Put all the sauce ingredients into a saucepan and bring to the boil. Turn the heat down and allow to simmer gently for 4 minutes. You should have a thick tomato sauce.
3. Put the mince, onions and salt and pepper in a bowl and mix together. Add just enough beaten egg to make the mince stick together. If you have a large egg you will not need all of it.
4. Form the mince into 4 burger shapes, about 2" thick.
5. Pour enough sauce into a casserole to cover the bottom. Place the burgers on the top and then spoon the rest of the sauce over the burgers.
6. Cook in the oven for 30 - 35 minutes.   If you are serving these burgers with rice, put it on to cook in about 15 minutes. Test one of the burgers to make sure that it is no longer pink in the middle. If it is not cooked, put back in the oven for another 5 minutes.
7. Serve with rice or jacket potatoes.

Meats

Lamb Cobbler ★★★

Serves 2   Preparation time 20 minutes, cooking time 30 minutes

Vegetarian option

Winter warmer, this recipe is a little fiddly, but it is inexpensive and filling. If you like the topping, it can be used, instead of potatoes, with other recipes such as Shepherds Pie or Monday Pie.

½ x 500g packet of mince, lamb or Quorn
I onion
I dessertspoon cooking oil
I x 14 oz/400g tin chopped tomatoes
I teaspoon mixed herbs
I tablespoon tomato puree
salt and pepper

Dumpling topping
I mug self raising flour
½ mug suet
½ mug water
pinch salt
I teaspoon freeze dried
basil or coriander

1. Preheat the oven to 180°C/gas reg 6.
2. Fry the onion in the oil until soft.
3. Add the mince and cook until the meat is no longer pink.
4. Add the tinned tomatoes, herbs, salt and pepper and tomato puree, stir well and simmer for 5 minutes.
5. Transfer to a casserole dish.
6. To make the dumpling top – put flour, suet, salt and herbs in a dish and stir well. Add the water, slowly, until it makes a soft ball.
7. Put some flour onto a board or plate, turn out the mixture and form a ball.
8. Cut into six pieces and form each into a ball.
9. Gently place them on the top of the meat mixture, brush the top with beaten egg or milk to help it brown. If you do not have a pastry brush use your fingers!
10. Bake for 25 - 30 minutes or until the crust is browned.

Beefy Mince and Pasta Bake ★

Serves 2 - 3   Preparation time 5 - 10 minutes, cooking time 20 - 25 minutes

Very simple to make and share with flat mates. It is OK reheated in the microwave but best eaten straight away.

Vegetarian option

1 x 14 oz/400g tin of Campbell's condensed tomato soup (undiluted)
¾ packet x 500g mince or Quorn
1 beef/vegetable stock cube
1½ mugs pasta
1 onion, chopped
1 teaspoon butter

½ mug grated cheese
2 cloves garlic, crushed
1 teaspoon freeze dried basil
salt and pepper

1. Preheat oven to 200°C/gas reg 7.
2. Cook the pasta (see page 12).
3. Fry the onion in the butter until soft.
4. Add the mince and cook until no longer pink.
5. Add the stock cube, tomato soup, garlic, herbs and salt and pepper.
6. Drain the pasta well and add to the meat mixture. Transfer to a casserole dish.
7. Top with grated cheese and cook for 20 - 25 minutes. The top should be browned.

Meats

Monday Pie ★ ★

Serves 2   Preparation time 10 minutes, cooking time 50 minutes.

Vegetarian option

This dish is easy to prepare and will make enough for two meals. It is fine microwaved the next day.

½ x 500g pack of beef, lamb or Quorn mince
1 onion, sliced
1 x 14 oz/400g tin baked beans
1 teaspoon butter
4 - 5 potatoes, washed and sliced
2 teaspoons Worcestershire sauce
1 stock cube, beef, lamb or vegetable, according to meat used.

1. Preheat the oven to 180°C/gas reg 6.
2. Fry the onion in the butter until soft.
3. Add the mince or Quorn and cook until the mince is no longer pink, or Quorn heated through.
4. Add crumbled stock cube, but no water, stir well. The cube will dissolve in the meat mixture.
5. Add the tin of beans and Worcestershire sauce and pour into a casserole dish.
6. Place the sliced potatoes on top of the meat in layers and cook for 50 minutes. Test the potatoes with a fork to check that they are cooked, if not, turn the oven down to 160°C/gas reg 4 and cook for another 10 minutes.

Lasagna ★ ★ ★ ★ ★

Serves 4   Preparation time 25 minutes, cooking time 25 minutes

Vegetarian option

Although this dish is a little complicated, it is not impossible for an inexperienced cook. Once you have mastered Spaghetti Bolognese and the quick cheese sauce, try this recipe when you have a few friends around.

Bolognese Sauce
- 1 x 500g pack of minced beef, lamb or Quorn
- 1 x 14 oz /400g tin chopped tomatoes
- 1 onion, chopped
- 1 dessertspoon cooking oil
- 2 cloves garlic, crushed
- 1 tablespoon tomato puree
- 1 stock cube
- 1 teaspoon mixed herbs
- salt and pepper

Quick Cheese Sauce
- 2 mugs grated cheese
- 2 tablespoons flour
- 2 mugs milk
- ½ teaspoon paprika
- ½ teaspoon nutmeg
- 2 teaspoons butter
- salt and pepper

1 x 250g packet of lasagna strips

1. Preheat the oven to 180°C/gas reg 6.
2. Make the cheese sauce (see page 23).
3. Make the Bolognese sauce (see page 41).
4. Use an oblong casserole dish; if you only have a round one you will need to break up the pasta strips to fit. First, put a layer of Bolognese sauce on the bottom of the dish and cover with some lasagna strips, making sure they do not overlap. Next, put a layer of cheese sauce, pasta strips, the rest of the Bolognese sauce, more pasta strips and then the rest of the cheese sauce. Finally, top with some grated cheese.
5. Cook for 25 minutes. Test the pasta with a fork to see if it is cooked through; if not, reduce the temperature of the oven to 160°C/gas reg 4 and cook for another 5 - 10 minutes. Serve with salad or garlic bread.

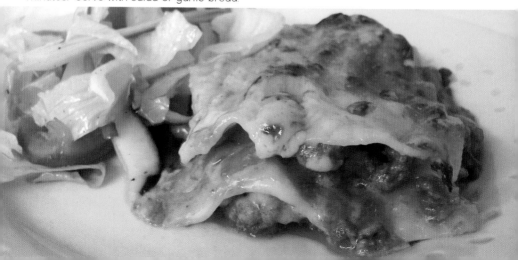

Spaghetti Bolognese ★★

Serves 2   Preparation and cooking time 20 minutes

Vegetarian option

'Spag Bol' is a must to master. If you cook enough sauce for two you can either share it with a flat mate or the next day add either curry paste or chilli and eat with rice or baked potatoes.

½ x 500g packet of mince, beef, lamb or Quorn
1 x 14 oz/400g tin chopped tomatoes
1 onion, chopped
1 teaspoon cooking oil
2 cloves garlic, chopped
1 tablespoon tomato puree
1 stock cube

1 teaspoon sugar
1 teaspoon freeze dried mixed herbs
1 glass red wine (if available)
4 - 5 mushroom, sliced (optional)
salt and pepper
. spaghetti

1. Fry the onion in the oil until soft.
2. Add the mince and cook until the meat is no longer pink.
3. Add the tin of tomatoes, tomato puree, mushrooms, garlic, sugar and wine. Crumble the stock cube into the pan, stir well. Bring to boil, then simmer gently for 10 minutes. Add the herbs one minute before the end of the cooking time and season well with salt and pepper.
4. Put spaghetti on to cook (see page 12 for how much and how to cook).
5. Drain the pasta and add a little butter or olive oil to stop it sticking together. Serve on plate with Bolognese sauce on the top. You can grate parmesan or cheddar cheese over the top if you like.

Mince Hot Pot ★ ★

Serves 2   Preparation time 15 minutes, cooking time 45 - 50 minutes

Vegetarian option

With this dish you get yummy roasted potatoes on top of tasty meat sauce. It is great microwaved the next day, so one cooking effort will give you two days meals.

½ x 500g packet of lamb, beef or Quorn mince
1 onion, chopped
3 - 4 mushrooms, sliced
1 x 14 oz/400g tin of chopped tomatoes
1 tablespoon tomato puree

oil to fry
4 - 5 thinly sliced potatoes
1 teaspoon freeze dried basil
1 stock cube, beef, lamb or vegetable.

1. Preheat the oven to 180°C/gas reg 6.
2. Fry the onion in the oil until soft.
3. Add the mince and cook until no longer pink.
4. Add the tomatoes, mushrooms, tomato puree and stock cube, bring to the boil and then transfer into a casserole dish.
5. Arrange the sliced, uncooked potatoes on the top, in layers, and brush the top with oil: fingers will work if you don't have a pastry brush.
6. Cook for 45 - 50 minutes, the potatoes should be browned on top. Check that the potatoes are cooked, if not, turn down oven to 160°C/gas reg 4 and cook for further 10 - 15 minutes.

Spicy Risotto ★★

Serves 1   Preparation and cooking time 20 minutes

Vegetarian option

This is a tasty dish. If you like hot food you can add more curry paste. It reheats well, so making double quantity is a good idea.

½ mug rice
1 mug water
½ pilau rice cube or 1 teaspoon pilau rice seasoning
¼ - ⅓ x 500g packet of lamb, beef or Quorn mince
1 small onion, chopped
2 mushrooms, sliced
1 clove garlic, chopped finely

½ lamb or vegetable stock cube
¼ mug water
1 teaspoon coriander leaves
2 teaspoons mild curry paste
1 teaspoon butter
salt and pepper

1. Cook rice with pilau rice cube (see page 13).
2. Fry the onion in the butter until the onions are soft.
3. Add the mince and cook until it is no longer pink.
4. Add the stock, curry paste, mushrooms, garlic and the ¼ mug of water, bring to the boil and simmer for 5 minutes or so until all the liquid has gone.
5. When the liquid has gone from the rice and it is cooked, transfer it to the meat mixture and add salt and pepper and the coriander leaves. Serve with some salad.

Beefburgers ★ ★

Makes 2 beefburgers
Preparation time 5 minutes, cooking time 10 minutes

Beefburgers don't have to be unhealthy. If you make them yourself from good quality mince, you will miss out on all the additives and preservatives that fast food chains put in.

oil to fry
½ x 500g pack of mince
1 egg, beaten
2 flat bread buns
any combination of lettuce, tomatoes, cucumber, gherkin etc..
mayo, tomato sauce or mustard

1. Mix the defrosted mince and the egg together. Season well with salt and pepper.
2. Divide the mixture into 2 and shape the burgers with your hands so they are about ¾" thick.
3. Heat a little oil in a frying pan. When hot, add the burgers. Cook for 4 - 5 minutes then carefully turn them over. Cook for a further 4 - 5 minutes.
4. Using a fork, check to see that the inside of the burger is cooked, i.e. that the meat is no longer pink. If not, cook longer, turning the burgers.
5. Put the cooked burger into the bread bun, add salad and the sauces to your taste.

Bobotie ★ ★

Serves 2   Preparation time 15 minutes, cooking time 40 minutes

This dish originates in South Africa. It has a very different taste and provides an interesting, tasty way to use mince. You can serve it with baked potatoes or salad. You can use the leftovers in sandwiches.

½ x 500g pack of minced beef
½ onion, chopped
1 clove garlic, finely chopped
oil to fry
2 teaspoons curry paste
½ an eating apple

⅓ mug of raisins
1 dessertspoon chutney, Branston pickle or similar
1 egg
1 mug milk
salt and pepper

1. Put the oven on to heat at 180°C/gas reg 6.
2. Fry the onions and garlic in a frying pan for 2 – 3 minutes.
3. Add the mince and cook until the meat is no longer pink.
4. Cut the apple into four and take out the core, chop the pieces into small chunks and add to the meat along with the curry paste, raisins, chutney, salt and pepper. Stir well and heat through for about 2 minutes. Pour into a greased casserole dish.
5. Beat the egg in a mug and add 1 mug of milk. Mix well and pour over the meat in the casserole dish.
6. Cook in the oven for 40 minutes, the egg mixture will set by then. Serve with jacket potatoes (see page 15) or salad.

Meats

Chilli Con Carne ★★

Serves 2   Preparation and cooking time 20 minutes

Vegetarian option

This is another standard dish which is useful to master. You can serve it with rice, jacket potatoes, pasta or crusty bread. If you are eating this meal by yourself you can reheat any leftovers the next day.

oil to fry
1 large onion, chopped
½ x 500g pack of mince, or Quorn
2 cloves garlic, finely chopped
1 stock cube, beef or lamb

1 x 14 oz/400g tin tomatoes
1 teaspoon chilli powder, more if you like it hot
1 x 14 oz/400g tin baked beans (you can use red kidney beans if you wish).

1. Fry the onion in the oil until soft. Add the garlic.
2. Add the mince and cook until the meat is no longer pink.
3. Add the tin of tomatoes and the stock cube.
4. Add the chilli powder and cook for 10 minutes.
5. Whilst the chilli is cooking, put the potatoes in the microwave on full power for 5 - 6 minutes. If you do not have a microwave you will need to put the potatoes in the oven (see page 15). You obviously need to put the potatoes in before you start cooking the chilli if you are using the oven! If you are using pasta or rice, put on to cook (see pages 12 & 13).
6. Add the beans to the chilli and cook for a further one minute. Taste to see if you would like more chilli powder. If you add more, cook for another minute.
7. Serve with the jacket potatoes, crusty bread, pasta or rice.

Quick Shepherds Pie ★ ★

Serves 2   Preparation time 20 minutes, cooking time 25 minutes

This is an easy way to make Shepherds Pie without using mashed potatoes. If you make enough for two this dish is ideal to reheat the next day.

½ x 500g pack of lamb, beef or Quorn mince
1 desertspoon gravy granules or Bisto
6 medium potatoes, cut into ½" cubes
½ mug water

salt and pepper
1 mug grated cheese
2 teaspoons butter

Vegetarian option

1. Preheat oven to 180°C/gas reg 6.
2. Put mince into a pan with the ½ mug water and bring to the boil. Simmer for 10 – 15 minutes.
3. Put diced potatoes in a separate pan with enough water to cover them, boil for 10 minutes and then drain. Add the butter and mix.
4. Add gravy powder to the meat; follow instructions on the packet of granules, as they differ according to brand. The gravy needs to be thickened to the consistency of double cream.   Season with salt and pepper.
5. Pour the mince into the bottom of a casserole dish.
6. Carefully spoon the potatoes on to the top and sprinkle with the cheese.
7. Cook for 20 – 25 minutes until the top is browned.

Easy Beef Stroganoff ★ ★ ★

Serves 2
Preparation time 15 - 20 minutes, cooking time 1 hour 30 minutes

Slightly more pricy dish but delicious. Everything but the wine is essential in this dish for it to taste right.

½ x 500g pack of cubed stewing beef or beef cut into thin strips
1 onion, chopped
1 tablespoon flour
1 mug yogurt or soured cream
2 teaspoons freeze dried basil or parsley
1 desertspoon Dijon mustard
glass white wine (optional)
2 cloves garlic, crushed

1 desertspoon cooking oil
1 beef stock cube
1 mug water
3 - 4 mushrooms
¼ teaspoon paprika
salt and pepper

1. Fry the onion in the oil.
2. Add the meat and cook on a medium heat until the meat is slightly browned, or until the outsides of the cubes are no longer pink.
3. Add the flour and stir well. Add the water (or wine + water to = 1 mug of liquid), stock cube, garlic, mustard, paprika and mushrooms and bring to the boil.
4. Simmer with a lid on the pan for 1½ hours. Check every 20 minutes to see that the sauce is not sticking on the bottom of the pan. Keep the heat quite low.
5. Remove from the heat and add the yogurt or soured cream and parsley.
6. Serve with rice and green vegetables, broccoli, green beans etc.

Lancashire Hot Pot ★ ★

Serves 2
Preparation time 5 - 10 minutes, cooking time 1 to 1½ hours

This is a very simple, appetising dish, quick to make and gives time for a little work while it cooks???!!

½ x 500g pack of cubed lamb, you could use lamb mince
2 onions, cut into 6 lengthways wedges

2 - 3 potatoes
2 carrots
3 cloves of garlic, finely chopped
1 lamb stock cube

2 mugs water
salt and pepper
2 tablespoons flour
1 desertspoon cooking oil to fry

1. Preheat the oven to 180°C/gas reg 6.
2. Fry the onions and garlic on a high heat until they brown slightly, add the meat and cook until the outside is no longer pink.
3. Add the flour and stir well.
4. Add the water and the stock cube, bring to the boil; the liquid should thicken.
5. Cut the carrots and potatoes into chunks and add to the mixture. Season with salt and pepper.
6. Transfer to a casserole dish with a lid and cook for 1 ½ hours. If you use lamb mince you will only need to cook for 1 hour.

Meats

Mexican Beef

Serves 2   Preparation time 15 minutes

If you have a little extra left in your food budget for the week, this is a good one to try. It is a little more expensive because you need to buy good quality beef steak otherwise the meat will not be tender.

½ onion, sliced
1 carrot, cut into thin slices
½ green or yellow pepper
1 clove garlic, finely chopped
250g rump steak cut into strips

1 x 7 oz/200g tin of chopped tomatoes
½ teaspoon chilli flakes
½ tablespoon tomato puree
oil to fry
salt and pepper

1. Fry the onions, carrots and garlic in the oil for 3 - 4 minutes, stirring frequently. Add the chopped pepper, cook for a further 4 - 5 minutes and then remove from the pan.
2. Add the thinly sliced beef to the pan and cook on a high heat for 4 - 5 minutes, stirring frequently until the meat is cooked.
3. Return the onions and pepper to the pan, add the tin of tomatoes, the tomato puree and the chilli and cook for 2 - 3 minutes.
4. Serve with rice. If you like things really hot, serve with salsa (see page 62).

Beef Stew ★★

Serves 2   Preparation Time 15 minutes, cooking time 1 1/2 hours

This is an old fashioned recipe, a good winter warmer. Using stewing beef means that it is a little more expensive, but it is delicious. Cooking the baking potatoes at the same time as the stew makes the meal simple and saves a bit of energy. Reheats well the next day.

1 dessertspoon of oil for frying
1 onion, cut into chunks
1 carrot, peeled and sliced
1 beef stock cube, dissolved in
a mug of hot water

350g cubed stewing steak
1 x 14 oz/400g tin of tomatoes
1 tablespoon flour
2 baking potatoes

1. Preheat the oven to 180°C/gas reg 6.
2. Fry the onions and carrots until they begin to brown. Add the meat and cook, stirring all the time, until it is no longer pink.
3. Sprinkle the flour over the ingredients in the pan. Stir for one minute making sure that the flour is evenly distributed.
4. Add the water and stock cube. Stir well, then add the tin of tomatoes. The sauce should thicken a little, but will thicken more as it cooks in the oven.
5. Place in a casserole dish, cover with a lid or foil and place in the oven for ¾ of an hour.
6. After ¾ of an hour, put the baking potatoes in the oven and cook everything for a further hour.

Meats

Hawaiian Risotto ★ ★

Serves 1   Cooking and preparation time 20 minutes

If you like the mix of sweet and savoury this is a dish for you, refreshingly different and delicious.

2 teaspoons butter
1 small onion, chopped
2 - 3 mushrooms, sliced
1 tomato, cut into chunks
1 slice of cooked ham, cut into pieces
¼ red pepper, sliced

1 egg
½ mug rice + ½ pilau rice cube (or seasoning)
2 pineapple slices, cut into pieces.
1 teaspoon soy sauce
1 teaspoon freeze dried coriander leaves
salt and pepper

1. Cook the rice with the pilau rice cube or seasoning.
2. Put a small amount of butter in a frying pan, beat the egg in a mug, put the pan on to heat. Once the butter is bubbling, add the egg to it and allow it to spread thinly over the base of the pan. It will cook in less than a minute. Once cooked, take out of the pan, cut into strips and leave to one side.
3. Fry the onions in the butter until soft.
4. Add the mushrooms and peppers and cook for 30 seconds.
5. Add the cooked rice (see page 13), pineapple chunks, soy sauce, ham, egg, tomato, and coriander leaves. Heat through gently. Season with salt and pepper.

Pasta with Cheesy Sauce and Ham ★★

Serves 1
Preparation and cooking time 15 minutes

Vegetarian option

This is a quick snack meal, its origins are in Italy, so you could always dream whilst you're eating it! If you are vegetarian you could add tofu to this recipe.

1 teaspoon butter
½ onion, chopped
2 mushrooms, sliced
½ mug grated cheese
1 mug milk

1 desertspoon flour
2 slices cooked ham, cut into pieces
¼ teaspoon paprika
¼ teaspoon basil or chives, freeze dried
¼ mug pasta
120g tofu (if you want the vegetarian option)

1. Cook the pasta, see page 12.
2. Fry the onion in the butter.
3. Add the flour, stir well and cook for 30 seconds.
4. Add the milk, cheese and paprika and stir well.   The mixture will thicken.
5. Add the ham or tofu, herbs and mushrooms and cook for one minute.
6. Drain the pasta well and stir everything together.

Pasta with Ham and Eggs ★ ★

Serves 2   Preparation and cooking time 15 - 20 minutes

This makes a quick and filling snack, you could keep most of the ingredients in your store cupboard.

pasta (tagliatelle, 2 'bunches')
2 slices of ham, more if it is thin ham
1 onion, chopped
1 teaspoon butter
3 - 4 mushrooms, sliced

1 desertspoon flour
1 hard boiled egg
½ mug milk + ½ mug of single cream
½ teaspoon freeze dried basil
salt and pepper

1. Put pasta on to boil (See page 12).
2. Fry onion in the butter.
3. Add the flour and stir well. Cook for 30 seconds.
4. Take off the heat and add the milk and cream, stir well and return to the heat. The mixture should thicken slightly.
5. Add the mushrooms, ham and basil and cook for 1 minute.
6. Cut the hard boiled egg into 4 and add. Don't stir too much or the egg will break up.
7. Drain the pasta, put on serving plate and pour the ham mixture over. Season with salt and pepper.

Pasta with Tomato Sauce *

Serves 1   Preparation time 10 minutes

Vegetarian option

Quick, easy, inexpensive lunch snack. You can replace the gammon with bacon or cooked ham.

1 teaspoon butter
1 small onion, chopped
1 clove garlic, crushed
½ mug pasta
1 medium slice of gammon, cut into pieces (optional for vegetarians)
2 mushrooms, sliced
1 x 7oz/200g tin chopped tomatoes
1 teaspoon tomato puree
½ teaspoon freeze dried mixed herbs
parmesan cheese (optional)
pepper

1. Cook pasta (see page 12).
2. Fry onions and the chopped gammon for 4 - 5 minutes.
3. Add mushrooms and garlic and cook for 1 minute.
4. Add the tinned tomatoes and herbs, simmer for 2 - 3 minutes, season with pepper (you will not need salt as the bacon or ham will be salty enough).
5. Drain the pasta and add a small amount of butter or olive oil to stop the pasta sticking together.
6. Mix the sauce and pasta together, sprinkle with parmesan if you wish.

Tortilla Wraps ★ ★

Each filling suggestion will fill 4 tortilla wraps.

Preparation time 10 - 15 minutes

Tortillas are traditionally Mexican, but have become so cosmopolitan you can fill them with an innumerable variety of ingredients! Here are a few suggestions for hot fillings. Tortillas are often served with salsa (see page 62) and sour cream.

Basic Recipe

4 tortilla wraps
I onion, sliced thinly
4 mushrooms, sliced thinly
I clove garlic, finely chopped
I red or green pepper, sliced thinly
I tablespoon tomato puree
½ teaspoon chilli flakes or chilli powder, you can add more or less according to your taste.
oil to fry

Vegetarian option

1. Heat the oil in a frying pan and add the onions and garlic, fry for 3 - 4 minutes then add the peppers and the mushrooms.
2. Add the tomato puree and the chilli, stir well and cook for a further 2 minutes to allow the flavours to mix.
3. Divide among the 4 wraps.

To this basic recipe you can add meats/ cheeses etc:

1. Chicken breast, cut into thin strips. Add to the onions once they have begun to cook. Allow the meat to cook before adding the peppers and the mushrooms.

2. If you want to add beef it needs to be lean steak. You do not need very much, a little will go a long way, so it does not need to cost lots. Fry the beef first and then put to one side while you fry the vegetables.

3. You can add grated cheese or feta cheese to the wrap but do not cook either. Put the hot food in the wrap and then sprinkle grated cheese or add chopped feta.

4. Tofu and Quorn are ideal to add to tortillas. If you are using hard tofu, add it to the pan along with the peppers. Quorn will need to be fried along with the onions.

Fun Foods

Variations

If you are vegetarian you can add a variety of vegetables to the basic recipe, such as:

courgettes, cut into thin strips
mange tout or sugar snaps, cut into half
peas
sweetcorn
bean sprouts
celery
butternut squash, cut into small pieces, boil for 5 minutes before adding at stage I.
beans, cannelini, pinto, haricot etc., make sure you rinse them well.
All these vegetables need to be added at stage I of the basic recipe, see opposite page.

Different flavourings

These move away from the traditional flavours, but if you really enjoy tortillas and find them convenient, try these ideas.

Replace the tomato puree and chillies with a teaspoon of curry paste.
Replace the chillies with barbecue sauce or Worcestershire Sauce.

Potato Wedges and Dips ★ ★

Preparation time 5 minutes, cooking time 25 minutes
This is excellent party, or video night food, easy to make, almost like mum's chips!

Wedges

2 medium potatoes per person
cooking oil
salt and pepper

Vegetarian

1. Preheat the oven to 200°C/gas reg 7.
2. Cut the potatoes in half, length ways, cutting each half into approximately 6 pieces, producing thin 'wedges'.
3. Oil a baking tray, you can use a casserole dish if it is large enough. Put the potatoes on it. Sprinkle more oil over the potatoes. Using your hands, toss the potatoes in the oil, making sure that every piece of potato is covered in oil. Drain off any excess; if you have too much oil the potatoes will not be crisp. Separate the wedges, leaving all the surfaces open to brown.
4. Season well with salt and pepper.
5. Cook for 25 - 30 minutes in a hot oven until potatoes are crisp and browned.

You can buy different flavourings in the supermarket for potato wedges, here are a few cheaper variations. Fill a mug ¼ full with oil and mix well with any of the following ingredients: crushed garlic, freeze dried herbs, rosemary, paprika (don't use too much as it is very hot), small quantities of curry powder or finely grated cheese.

Fun Foods

Preparation time 5 - 10 minutes.   Each of these dip recipes will serve 3 people.

You can buy packets of dips in the supermarket. Here are a few ideas which are slightly less expensive and you can make them whilst the wedges are cooking.

1. 1 x 200/250g carton of soured cream with ½ mug finely grated cheese and 1 teaspoon of mustard. Mix together and season with salt and pepper.

2. Plain yogurt, mixed with ¼ cucumber, chopped; ½ onion, finely chopped; 1 teaspoon freeze dried mint.

3. 1 x 200/250g carton soured cream or creme frais, mixed with 2 cloves garlic, very finely chopped; 2 spring onions, finely chopped; and 1 tablespoon of lemon juice.

4. 1 x 200/250g carton creme frais, mixed with 2 teaspoons tomato puree; 3 - 4 drops of tobasco sauce or 2 teaspoons chilli sauce; and 1 teaspoon sugar.

5. Small carton of plain yogurt mixed with ½ mug mayonnaise; together with the grated rind and juice of a lime. Season with salt and pepper.

6. Small carton of soured cream, mixed with 5 - 6 spring onions, chopped; ½ mug finely grated cheese; 1 teaspoon of freeze dried chives; salt and pepper.

7. 1 x 250g pack of cream cheese mixed with 1 teaspoon chilli sauce. Add more chilli if you like it hot!

clockwise from the top left - yogurt and cucumber, soured cream and cheese, cheese and onion, fromage frais with chilli

These dips can be used if you have a party. Use carrot sticks, celery sticks, spicy crisps or cheese straws.

Nachos ★

Serves 2 - 3   Preparation time 3 minutes, cooking time 2 minutes

Vegetarian

Nachos are so quick to make and are excellent for parties or snacks while you are relaxing, watching a video etc..

½ x 200g packet of corn chips, plain or flavoured
1½ mugs of grated cheese
1 x 375g jar of salsa sauce or recipe on page 62

1. Heat the oven to 220°C/gas reg 9.
2. Pile the chips on an ovenproof plate.
3. Sprinkle the grated cheese on the top and cover the chips.
4. Place in the oven for 2 - 3 minutes only, the cheese only needs to melt, it does not need to brown.
5. Pour the salsa over the top, serve and eat immediately.

Fun Food

Mini Pizzas ★★

For 4 hungry people.   Preparation and cooking time 20 minutes

These make great every day food, as well as good, inexpensive party food. They are very simple to make and there are endless variations of toppings.

Basic tomato sauce

I small onion, chopped
I clove garlic, chopped finely
I x 14 oz/200g tin chopped tomatoes
I teaspoon freeze dried mixed herbs
I tablespoon tomato puree
I teaspoon sugar
oil to fry
salt and pepper

Fry the onions and garlic in the oil until the onions begin to brown. Add the tinned tomatoes, tomato puree, and sugar. Bring to the boil and allow to cook briskly for about 5 minutes, stirring frequently. This will cause the juice to boil down and thicken a little. Add the herbs and season with salt and pepper.

4 muffins
400g Mozzarella cheese.

1. Make the basic tomato sauce. See above.
2. Put the grill on to heat up.
3. Cut the muffins in half, horizontally.
4. Divide the tomato sauce between the muffins.
5. Arrange the various toppings on the muffins.
6. Grate the mozzarella cheese and sprinkle liberally on top.
7. Using a slotted turner, transfer the muffins to the grill pan. Cook under the grill until the cheese begins to bubble and brown.

Toppings

pepperoni or salami
sundried tomatoes
mushrooms
peppers

ham
pineapple
peppers

tuna
sweetcorn

sundried tomatoes
anchovies

sundried tomatoes
mushrooms
olives

red beans
mushrooms
peppers

Salsa ★

Preparation time 10 minutes

Vegetarian

Salsa is very easy to make! You can buy salsa in jars in the supermarket, but they will not taste as good as these. If you are having a party these will work out much cheaper than the bought variety. Salsa is good with tortilla chips, quesidillas, and big wraps.

Avocado Salsa
1 medium avocado, peeled and chopped into small pieces.
1 medium onion, finely chopped
2 medium tomatoes, chopped into small pieces
½ teaspoon chilli powder
¼ teaspoon paprika
½ teaspoon sugar
1 teaspoon lemon juice (this stops the avocado from discolouring)
salt and pepper

Prepare all the ingredients and mix together.

Front - avocado salsa, back - tomato and onion

Tomato and onion salsa
4 tomatoes, cut into small pieces
1 green chilli pepper, chopped finely
½ onion, chopped finely
1 teaspoon sugar
1 teaspoon lemon juice
Salt and Pepper

Prepare ingredients and mix together.

If you like your salsa really hot, then adjust the amount of chilli powder or chilli flakes. Fresh chillies always make a better flavour, but powder and flakes are fine to use. If you use fresh chillies, do be careful to wash your hands well after chopping them, and don't touch around your eyes!

Dipping salsa
1 teaspoon oil to fry
1 x 14 oz/400g tin of chopped tomatoes
1 onion, finely chopped
3 cloves garlic, finely chopped
1 teaspoon sugar
½ tablespoon tomato puree
½ teaspoon paprika
1 teaspoon chilli flakes
2 teaspoon freeze dried chives

1. Fry the onions and garlic in a pan until they begin to brown.
2. Add the tin of tomatoes and bring to the boil. Add the tomato puree, chilli, paprika and sugar. Simmer gently for 3 - 4 minutes.

Dipping salsa

Fun Food

Quesidillas ★★

Vegetarian options

Quesidillas can be varied. Here are the basic instructions and one set of ingredients which can be used. If you are vegetarian, obviously leave out the meat and add other vegetables of your choice. It is best to buy the soft flour tortillas for quesidillas.

1 x 14 oz/400g can of canellini beans
1 chicken breast or 200g beef steak
8 tortilla (soft flour) wraps

1 onion, chopped finely
1 pepper, chopped
5 mushrooms, sliced

1. Wash the beans well and leave to drain.
2. Fry the whole chicken or beef in a little oil until cooked through (no longer pink inside) Take out of pan and leave to stand.
3. Fry the onion until it begins to brown, then add the pepper and mushrooms. Cook for another 3 - 4 minutes. Take off the heat.
4. Cut the chicken or beef into thin strips and add to the vegetable mix. Season well with salt and pepper. Place in a bowl.
5. Put the grill on to heat up.
6. Wash the frying pan. Butter one side of the tortilla wraps. Put the freshly cleaned pan on to heat up. Put one of the wraps, butter side down, in the pan. Put ¼ of the filling onto the wrap and spread it out, then place the other wrap, butter side up, on the top of the filling. Now place under the grill until the butter begins to brown.
7. Slide onto a plate and cut into wedges. Serve with salsa (see page 62) and/or soured cream.

Fun Foods

Big Wraps ★★

Makes 4   Preparation time 15 minutes

This is the kind of recipe you can add and take away ingredients to suit your taste. You can use leftover cooked meat, and spice things up if you want to, by adding chilli sauce or curry paste to the pan before you add the rice. There are enough tasty ingredients for you to leave out the meat if you are vegetarian.

4 tortilla wraps
½ mug of cooked rice (see page 13)
1 onion, finely chopped
1 red, green or yellow pepper, chopped
4 mushrooms, cut into fairly small pieces
1 chicken breast, cut into small pieces
or ¼ x 500g pack of mince

½ mug of finely grated strong cheddar cheese
1 small tin of sweetcorn
oil to fry
salt and pepper
a few cocktail sticks.
Salsa (see page 62)

Vegetarian option

1. Prepare all the ingredients.
2. Fry the onions in oil for 2 - 3 minutes until they begin to soften. Add the mushrooms and pepper and continue to cook for about 5 minutes.
3. Add the meat and cook until it is no longer pink.
4. Add the rice and the drained sweetcorn and cook for 3 - 4 minutes until everything is heated through. Season with salt and pepper. Take off the heat and leave in the pan to keep warm.
5. Gently warm the tortilla wraps under the grill on low heat for 2 minutes or in the microwave for 10 seconds.
6. Place a wrap on a plate and put ¼ of the filling onto it and sprinkle the grated cheese on the top. Fold the tortilla over and secure with a cocktail stick. If you don't have any, just roll the wrap over.
You will need to eat this with a knife and fork, not really possible with your fingers, but you could always give it a go if you don't mind the mess! Serve with salsa.

64

Chicken Casserole ★ ★

Serves 2   Preparation time 10 minutes, cooking time 1 hour

Quick and easy to prepare, leave it in the oven whilst you relax. If you want to use 'cook in sauces' with chicken thighs, follow this recipe to stage 2 but omit the flour and add the sauce.

4 chicken thighs
1 onion, chopped
4 - 5 mushrooms, sliced
2 cloves garlic, finely chopped
2 teaspoons flour

oil to fry
1 x 14oz/400g tin chopped tomatoes
2 teaspoons Worcestershire sauce
1 teaspoon mixed herbs

1. Preheat oven to 180°C/gas reg 6.
2. Fry the chicken until brown on both sides, transfer into a casserole dish.
3. Fry the onions until soft. Sprinkle the flour in and stir well.
4. Add the tin of tomatoes, garlic, mushrooms, Worcestershire sauce and herbs.
5. Bring to the boil and then transfer to the casserole. Put a lid on and bake for 1 hour.
6. Serve with rice or baked potatoes and green vegetables.

Baked Chicken Topped with Cheese ★ ★

Serves 2   Preparation time 15 minutes, cooking time 1 hour

Looks more complicated than it is. You must use chicken breast, as legs and thighs will not cook in the time. This recipe gives a change of texture from the majority of sauce-based dishes.

1 dessertspoon milk
1 teaspoon mustard
½ mug grated cheese
1½ dessertspoons flour

1 teaspoon chopped chives
2 chicken breasts
2 large potatoes

1. Put potatoes on to bake, oven 200°C/gas reg 7.
2. Mix milk and mustard together.
3. Mix together the grated cheese, flour and chives.
4. Dip the chicken breasts in the milk and then into the cheese mixture.
5. Place on a baking tray or the bottom of a casserole dish and pile the remaining cheese mixture on the top. Leave until the potatoes have 30 minutes left to cook.
6. Bake in the oven, with the potatoes, for 30 - 35 minutes. The cheese should be browned when done.
7. Serve with salad.

Creamy Chicken ★ ★

Serves 1   Preparation and cooking time 20 minutes

This recipe is a little more expensive, but is very easy to cook and delicious.

1 chicken breast, cut into pieces
½ onion, chopped
1 teaspoon butter
¼ pint double cream
½ teaspoon freeze dried basil

1 clove garlic, finely chopped
1 chicken stock cube, crumbled
2 - 3 mushrooms, sliced
rice to serve.

1. Put rice on to cook with ½ pilau rice cube or pilau seasoning (see page 13).
2. Fry onions in the butter until soft.
3. Add the chicken breast and the garlic, cook on a high heat until the chicken is no longer pink. Add the mushrooms and cook for 2 minutes.
4. Add the cream and the stock cube, cook gently for 5 - 10 minutes, stirring occasionally.
5. Add the basil, cook for one minute.
6. Serve with rice.

Chicken Curry ★★

Serves 2   Preparation and cooking time 20 minutes

If you use chicken thighs in this recipe, pre-cook them in the oven for 50 minutes in a casserole dish with a little water and salt and pepper. You can use leftover, cooked chicken or replace the chicken with mince, beef lamb or Quorn.

2 chicken breasts
1 onion, chopped
1 dessertspoon cooking oil
2 teaspoons flour
3 cloves garlic, finely chopped
4 teaspoons mild curry paste (use less if the curry paste is hot)

1 potato, cut into ½ "cubes
1 mug water
1 chicken stock cube, crumbled
½ mug natural yogurt

1. Fry the onion and potato in the oil.
2. Cut the chicken breasts into pieces and add to the pan. Cook for 2 - 3 minutes until the chicken is no longer pink on the outside.
3. Add the flour and stir well. Add the garlic, water, curry paste and stock cube, stir well.
4. Bring to the boil and then simmer for 10 - 15 minutes until the chicken and the vegetables are cooked.
5. Stir in the yogurt but do not let it boil. Cook gently for 1 minute.
6. Serve with rice (see page 13).

Sweet and Sour Chicken ★★

Serves 2   Preparation time 20 minutes

This sweet and sour recipe can be used with a variety of things: meatballs (see page 75), cooked sausages, cooked beef, and fish.

butter or oil for frying
1 onion, chopped
2 chicken breasts, cut into pieces
4 mushrooms, sliced
½ red pepper, sliced
1 clove garlic, chopped finely

Sweet and sour Sauce

2 tablespoons tomato puree
3 tablespoons sugar
2 tablespoons white wine vinegar
1 tablespoon soy sauce
2 teaspoons cornflour
1 mug water

1. Put the rice on to cook (see page 13).
2. To make the sauce, put all the sauce ingredients in a saucepan, apart from the cornflour. Bring to the boil, stirring well. Mix the cornflour with a little cold water and pour into the sauce, stirring as you do. The sauce should thicken. Leave the sauce off the heat until you have cooked the chicken.
3. Fry the onion, garlic, mushrooms and pepper for 1 minute. Add the chicken pieces and cook for another 5 minutes, stirring frequently.
4. Add the sweet and sour sauce to the pan, bring to the boil, turn down the heat and simmer for 5 minutes.
5. Serve with rice.

Roast Chicken ★

Serves 2   Preparation time 5 minutes, cooking time 1 hour 45 minutes

This recipe is for two people. If you just cook for yourself, use less vegetables and the leftover chicken can be used the next day, either in sandwiches, risotto or pasta dishes.

1 onion, red or white
1 small chicken, approximately 1.5 Kg
3 large potatoes
cooking oil

1. Put oven on to 180°C/gas reg 6.
2. Wash potatoes and cut into large pieces.
3. Peel the onion and cut into 6 wedges.
4. Remove any giblets from inside the chicken and discard. Place the chicken in an oiled, flat, roasting dish or a casserole dish. Add the potatoes and the onion and brush with oil. Sprinkle a little salt over and, if you wish, add some rosemary. Cover with a lid or foil.
5. Cook for 1 hour, if you have a larger chicken, then cook for longer.
6. Take the lid or foil from the chicken and cook for a further 25 - 45 minutes to allow everything to brown.
7. Serve with vegetables.

Chicken Drumsticks ★

Serves 2   Preparation time 5 - 10 minutes, cooking time 40 minutes

Look out for bargain offers in the supermarket. Buy a quantity of drumsticks, if you want to use them in small amounts, then separate them before you put them in your freezer. Larger quantities are useful for parties or just when you have a few friends around.

4 chicken legs
1 teaspoon mustard
2 teaspoon Worcestershire sauce
½ teaspoon brown sugar
1 tablespoon tomato sauce
salt and pepper

1. Preheat oven to 180°C/gas reg 6.
2. Mix together the mustard, tomato sauce, Worcestershire sauce, salt, pepper and sugar.
3. Baste (spread over with a spoon) the chicken legs with half the liquid.
4. Place on an oiled baking tray or casserole dish. Bake for 20 minutes.
5. Baste legs with the rest of the liquid and bake for another 20 minutes.
6. Serve with salad and bread rolls.

Pasta and Chicken Bake ★ ★

Serves 2   Preparation time 15 minutes, cooking time 25 minutes

I red onion, finely chopped
2 teaspoon lemon juice
4 small mushrooms, sliced
2 chicken breasts
oil to fry
I mug pasta

¼ mug raisins
I x 250g packet of low fat soft cheese with garlic and herbs
½ mug of grated mozzarella or cheddar cheese
salt and pepper

1. Preheat the oven to 180°C/gas reg 6.
2. Heat the oil in a frying pan and add the chicken breasts. Cook on a high heat for 2 minutes, turn over and cook the other side for 2 minutes. Turn down the heat and cook for another 5 minutes. Take off the heat and cut into strips.
3. Add the onions and mushrooms to the pan and cook for 4 – 5 minutes until the onions are softened.
4. Cook the pasta (see page 12) and drain well. Return to the pan you cooked it in.
5. Break up the soft cheese with a fork and add to the pasta, the warmth of the pan will cause the cheese to melt slightly.
6. Add the chicken, the raisins and the lemon juice, season with salt and pepper and pour into a casserole dish. Sprinkle the grated mozzarella over the top. Bake in the oven for 20 – 25 minutes until golden brown.

                                                                    Chicken

Chicken Risotto ★ ★

Serves 1   Preparation time 15 minutes, cooking time 15 minutes

This dish is great eaten cold, so you could double the quantity and eat half with salad the next day.

1 chicken breast or 2 - 3 small chicken fillets
⅓ mug rice, can be risotto or basmati
¼ red pepper, chopped
2 mushrooms, sliced
1 onion, chopped

½ teaspoon mild curry paste
½ chicken stock cube, crumbled
¼ tin sweetcorn
1 mug water
1 teaspoon freeze dried chives

1. Fry the onion until soft.
2. Cut the chicken into bite sized pieces, add to the frying pan and fry for 2 - 3 minutes until the outside is no longer pink.
3. Add the mushroom and pepper.
4. Add the rice (uncooked), stock cube, curry paste and water, simmer gently for 20 minutes, stirring from time to time. Add more water if the mixture has dried up before the rice is cooked. There should be very little liquid left when the dish is finished.
5. Add the sweetcorn and chives, heat through and serve.

Chicken

Chicken Hot Pot ★

Serves 2   Preparation time 5 minutes, cooking time 1 hour 30 minutes

As you can see from the preparation time, this recipe is very easy. You will have to wait for it to cook, it just needs a bit of forward planning. You can add other flavourings to the stock e.g. 2 teaspoons curry paste or 1 teaspoon chilli paste. You can also replace the stock with a 'cook in sauce', but you will need to add some water as the 'cook in sauce' will dry up during the longer cooking time.

4 chicken thighs, skins removed
1 mug hot water
1 chicken stock cube
3 carrots, washed and sliced
3 large potatoes, washed and cut into chunks

1 onion, cut into 6 wedges
2 cloves garlic, chopped
salt and pepper

1. Preheat oven to 190°C/gas reg 7.
2. Put the stock cube in a mug, fill up with the hot water and stir until the cube has dissolved.
3. Put all the ingredients in a casserole dish, season with salt and pepper.
4. Pour the stock into the casserole dish.
5. Cover with a lid or foil, and cook for 1 hour 30 minutes.
6. You can take the lid off for the last half hour to let things brown a little.

Spicy Chicken Meatballs ★ ★ ★

Serves 2   Preparation and cooking time 25 minutes

This dish is a little more difficult, try it after you have gained a bit of experience in cooking. You need to use fresh chillies, dried ones will not taste the same.

½ lb or 200g minced chicken
or 4 small fillets, chopped finely
2 spring onions, chopped finely
I small red chilli, chopped finely
½ can sweetcorn
salt and pepper
oil to fry

Sweet and sour sauce
I mug water
2 tablespoons tomato puree
3 tablespoons sugar
2 tablespoons white wine
vinegar
I tablespoon soy sauce
2 teaspoons cornflour

rice to serve

1. To make the sauce - put all ingredients, except the cornflour, into a saucepan and bring to the boil. Mix the cornflour with a little water, add to the sauce: the mixture should thicken slightly. Leave until you have cooked the rest of the dish.
2. Put the rice on to cook (see page 13) whilst you make the meatballs.
3. Mix the thawed chicken, spring onions, chilli, sweetcorn, salt and pepper together in a dish or bowl. Take care not to touch your face or eyes after chopping the chilli, wash your hands well.
4. Put a little flour on a board or plate and make small balls from the meat mixture. Use flour to stop the mixture sticking to your fingers.
5. Put a little oil in the frying pan and put the balls in, keep the heat at a medium level for 5 - 10 minutes. Turn the balls frequently, two forks will be the best tools for this.
6. Check to see if they are cooked by cutting through one of the meatballs: if the meat is no longer pink then they are ready.
7. Serve with rice and the sweet and sour sauce.

Chicken

Tim's Special Mango Chicken ★★

Serves 2 - 3   Preparation and cooking time 20 minutes

Tim, my youngest son, insisted this recipe should go in the new edition. This is one of his favourite meals to cook. We have cooked it together for 25 people. Simply multiply the recipe accordingly. Although mango pulp is a bit unusual and tricky to find it is usually available at supermarkets and well worth the search. You can eat this with rice and naan bread, or serve with jacket or roast potatoes and vegetables; carrots, mange tout, green beans etc.

2 chicken breasts, cut into bite size pieces
4 - 5 spring onions, you could use 1 medium onion
1 teaspoon whole grain mustard
2 teaspoons curry paste
1 mug mango pulp
1 tablespoon soured cream
1 clove garlic, chopped finely

1. Fry the chicken for 2 minutes, then add the onions and garlic. Fry for another 2 minutes, stirring continuously.
2. Add the mango pulp, curry paste and mustard. Cook for a further 3 - 4 minutes over a medium heat.
3. Take the pan off the heat and stir in the soured cream.
4. Serve with rice and vegetables.

Lemon Chicken ★

Serves 2   Preparation and cooking time 15 minutes

This dish is incredibly easy to make and tastes delicious. This recipe will cost a fraction of the price you would pay for a 'takeaway'.

1 teaspoon oil to fry
2 whole chicken breasts
1 lemon
2 spring onions

Sauce
1 heaped teaspoon cornflour
¾ mug cold water
juice of a lemon
3 dessertspoons sugar

1. Mix the sauce ingredients together until smooth. Slice the other lemon as seen in the picture. Cut the spring onions into small strips, as above.
2. Heat the oil in the frying pan. Add the whole chicken breasts. Cook on a high heat until each side is browned. Turn the heat down to medium and cook for a further 5 minutes. Check to see that the meat is cooked through, if so remove from the pan and place on a serving dish.
3. Stir the sauce ingredients again and then add to the pan. Stir until the sauce comes to the boil, it should thicken. Add the slices of lemon and heat them over a gentle heat for 1 minute. Take off the heat.
4. Cut the chicken breasts into slices. Arrange the lemon slices on top and pour the sauce over.
5. Serve with rice and vegetables. Mange Tout or sugar snaps will go well with this dish.

Chicken Noodles **

Serves 1   Preparation time 10 minutes

This is nearly as quick as pot noodle but much more nutritious and appetising.

¼ x 250g pack of egg noodles
oil to fry
one chicken breast or three small chicken fillets
2 spring onions, sliced
½ chicken stock cube, dissolved in ½ mug boiling water
1 teaspoon soy sauce
¼ red pepper
salt and pepper

1. Cover the noodles with boiling water and leave to stand for 4 minutes.
2. Cut the chicken into bite size pieces and fry in the oil.
3. Add the onion and pepper and fry for 2 minutes.
4. Add the stock and the soy sauce together with the drained noodles and cook for 1 minute.
5. Serve.

Noodle Omelette ★ ★

Serves 2   Preparation and cooking time 10 - 15 minutes

Vegetarian options

This recipe is very versatile. If you are vegetarian you can add different cooked vegetables or tofu at stage 5; alternatively, for those of you who eat everything, you could add flaked tuna, ham cut into pieces, baked beans, crispy bacon, cooked chicken pieces and almost anything!

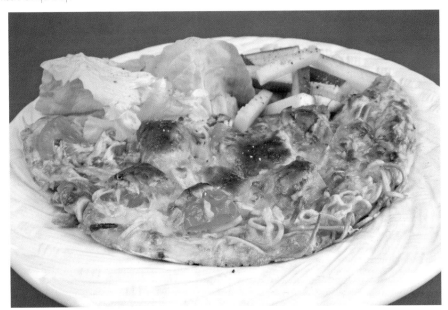

¼ x 250g packet of egg noodles
I onion, chopped
I dessertspoon soy sauce
I teaspoon freeze dried chives
4 eggs, beaten in a mug with I desertspoon water.

½ teaspoon chives or mixed herbs
I large tomato, cut into pieces
½ mug grated cheese
butter to fry

1. Pour boiling water over the noodles, leave for 4 minutes. Put grill on to heat up.
2. Using a frying pan, fry the onions in the butter, allowing them to brown a little.
3. Drain the noodles well and add to the frying pan, spreading them over the base of the pan. Allow them to fry a little, don't stir them.
4. Add the soy sauce and sprinkle the herbs over the noodles and add the tomatoes.
5. Add the beaten eggs and sprinkle the grated cheese over the top. Allow to cook in the pan for 3 - 4 minutes, keeping the pan on a medium heat. This will allow the base of the omelette to brown slightly, whilst the egg on the top may still be quite runny. Do not stir the omelette!
6. Put the frying pan, with the omelette in it, under a hot grill, take care not to burn the handle of the pan. Grill until the cheese is brown and the top of the egg is cooked. Serve with salad.

Vegetarian

Vegetable Stir Fry ★

Serves 2   Preparation and cooking time 25 minutes

Vegetarian

Do not worry if you don't have a wok for frying; either a larger saucepan or your frying pan will work just as well. You can vary the vegetables used. Remember to add the ones that need cooking the longest at stage 1.

oil to fry
1 onion, chopped
1 small aubergine, sliced
1 courgette, sliced
4 mushrooms, sliced
1 clove garlic, chopped finely

1 x 14 oz/400g can chopped tomatoes
2 tablespoons soy sauce
1 tablespoon tomato puree
salt and pepper
1 teaspoon freeze dried basil

1. Cut up the aubergine and fry with the onion in the oil.
2. Add the garlic, tin of tomatoes, soy sauce, ½ mug of water and cook for 5 minutes.
3. Add the courgette and mushrooms, soy sauce and tomato puree and cook for a further 10 minutes, stirring occasionally. Add more water if necessary.
4. Add the basil, season with salt and pepper and cook for 1 minute and serve with fresh crusty bread or toast.

Vegetarian

Vegetable Curry ★ ★

Serves 2   Preparation and cooking time 20 minutes

You can add and take away vegetables from this recipe depending what you have to hand. Make sure that the vegetables which take longest to cook go in at the beginning, carrots and potatoes, for example. Mushrooms, cauliflower and broccoli types need to go in towards the end!

Vegetarian

oil to fry
2 cloves garlic, chopped finely
1 onion, chopped
1 courgette, sliced
1 x 14oz/400g can chick peas
1 potato, cubed
4 mushrooms, sliced
veg stock cube, crumbled

1 mug water
1 tablespoon tomato puree
¼ mug sultanas
1 eating apple, cut into medium chunks
2 tablespoons curry paste, depending on taste

Mint Raita
¼ pint yogurt, creme frais or soured cream
1 tablespoon fresh mint or 2 teaspoons freeze dried

1. Fry the onion in the oil until soft.
2. Add the garlic, apple and potatoes, cook in the oil for 2 - 3 minutes.
3. Add the water and stock cube, bring to the boil and then simmer for 10 minutes.
4. Add the courgette, sultanas, mushrooms, tomato puree and curry paste. You may need to add a little more water. Cook for 5 minutes.
5. Add the chick peas and cook for 2 minutes.
6. Serve with rice.
7. To make the Raita, just add the mint to the yogurt, this will cool the curry down if you have put too much curry paste in! It also adds a good contrast to the flavour of the curry.

Vegetable Toad in the Hole ★★★

Serves 2   Preparation time 20 minutes, cooking time 30 - 35 minutes

The secret of good Toad In The Hole is a hot oven and hot fat! Non-vegetarians may wish to replace all the vegetables with sausages!

Vegetarian

Batter
1 mug plain flour
3 eggs, beaten
½ mug milk + 1 mug water
2 tablespoons white Flora or oil
pinch of salt

butter to fry
1 clove garlic, finely chopped
1 onion, cut into chunks
2 carrots, sliced
6 - 8 green beans
a few florets of broccoli
2 tomatoes, cut into chunks
4 - 5 mushrooms, cut in half
1 teaspoon freeze dried mixed herbs
salt and pepper.

1. Put the flour in the bowl and add the eggs, salt and a little of the milk. Mix well, beat with a whisk or a large spoon. Add enough milk and water (in equal amounts) to make the mixture look like single cream.
2. Put enough white Flora or oil in the bottom of a large casserole dish or deep baking tray to cover the bottom. Put in a hot oven 220°C/gas reg 9.
3. Boil the carrots and green beans in a little water. Leave cooking while you fry the onions and the garlic. Add the broccoli to the boiling vegetables after 5 minutes or so. Boil for a further 5 minutes and then drain all the vegetables.
4. Add the tomatoes, mushrooms, mixed herbs and the cooked, drained vegetables to the frying pan and stir. Season with salt and pepper. Leave off the heat. Drain the boiled vegetables.
5. By now the fat should be very hot; it is best if it is smoking slightly. Carefully take out of the oven, pour the batter in, it should bubble around the edges as you pour it in. Carefully pour the vegetables on the top and spread them out. If you are using sausages you do not need to cook them, just add them in raw, but they must be defrosted.
6. Place the dish back in the oven, cook for 30 - 35 minutes or until browned. The mixture should rise around the edges. If the top of the 'toad' begins to get too browned before the centre is cooked, turn down the temperature of the oven.

Vegetarian

Vegetable Bake ★ ★ ★

Serves 2   Preparation time 15 minutes, cooking time 20 minutes

Vegetarian

You can use any mixture of vegetables for this dish. Make sure that there are some that you can fry at the beginning, as this gives more taste. Boil the vegetables which take longer to cook, carrots, potatoes, parsnips etc.

1 desertspoon cooking oil
1 onion, chopped
1 carrot, sliced
1 courgette, sliced
4 mushrooms, sliced
1 sweet potato, cut into chunks
½ mug frozen peas

½ red or green pepper, sliced
small head of broccoli, broken into florets
2 x Quick cheese sauce (see page 23)
2 teaspoons Worcestershire sauce
salt and pepper
½ mug grated cheese

1. Preheat oven to 180°C/gas reg 6.
2. Place the carrots and sweet potato in a pan, cover with water and bring to the boil. Simmer for 5 minutes and add the broccoli and peas. Cook for another 5 minutes. Drain well.
3. Fry onions until soft, add mushrooms, peppers and courgettes. Cook for 2 minutes.
4. Mix all the vegetables together, place in a casserole dish, sprinkle with the Worcestershire sauce.
5. Make a double quantity of Quick Cheese Sauce and pour over the vegetables.
6. Sprinkle the grated cheese over the top and bake in the oven for 20 - 25 minutes. The cheese should be browned on top.

Nut and Potato Roast ★ ★

Serves 2

Preparation time 10 - 15 minutes, cooking time 40 minutes

Vegetarian

2 medium potatoes
200g packet of mixed, chopped nuts
1 small onion, chopped finely
1 clove garlic, chopped
3 mushrooms, chopped finely
1 tablespoon butter for frying
2 eggs, beaten
½ x 200g tub of full fat soft cheese
1 teaspoon dried herbs, basil, chives or mixed herbs

1. Put oven on to preheat, 180°C/gas reg 6. Grease a casserole dish.
2. Peel the potatoes and cut into chunks, boil for 10 - 15 minutes until cooked. Drain and mash with a fork.
3. Fry the chopped onions in a pan until they begin to soften.   Add the garlic and mushrooms and continue to cook for another 2 - 3 minutes. Season well with salt and pepper. Take off the heat. Add the cheese, the heat from the onions will help it to mix in. Add the nuts, potatoes, herbs and eggs.
4. Pour into the casserole dish and cook for 40 minutes. The roast should brown on the top.
5. Serve hot with salad or with baked potatoes. If you want to spice it up a little, serve with salsa.

Classic Nut Roast ★ ★

Serves 2   Preparation time 10 minutes, cooking time 20 minutes

Vegetarian

You can use a variety of nuts in this recipe, but cashews, macadamians or Brazil nuts seem to work the best, as they have a slightly sweeter taste than some other nuts.

I small onion, chopped finely
I x 200g chopped cashew nuts
2 mushrooms, chopped finely
2 slices wholemeal bread

½ mug vegetable stock
I teaspoon Marmite
I teaspoon mixed herbs

1. Preheat the oven to 180°C/gas reg 6. Grease a small ovenproof dish - you can use your casserole dish.
2. Fry the onions in a little oil until they begin to brown, add the mushrooms and cook for a further 2 - 3 minutes. Take off the heat.
3. Chop the nuts if necessary. Add to the pan.
4. Make the bread into breadcrumbs. Just rub it between your fingers, it does not matter if the breadcrumbs are a bit chunky. Add to the pan.
5. Using ½ mug of boiling water, add ½ vegetable stock cube to make up the stock. Add the teaspoon of Marmite and stir until dissolved.
6. Add to the pan along with the herbs. Mix everything together.
7. Pour into the dish and cook for 20 minutes. If you double the quantity, you will need to cook for another 5 minutes. The nuts should be brown on top.

Vegetarian

Serves 2
Preparation time 10 minutes, cooking time 10 minutes

Vegetarian

The cauliflower and broccoli make a good combination of flavours. If you are not a vegetarian, then you can serve this dish with crispy grilled bacon or sausages.

Double quantity of Quick Cheese Sauce (see page 23)
1 small cauliflower, broken into florets
1 small piece of broccoli, broken into florets
½ mug grated cheese.

1. Preheat oven to 200°C/gas reg 7.
2. Cook the cauliflower and broccoli for 5 - 7 minutes (see page 11).
3. Make the Quick Cheese Sauce (see page 23).
4. Put on a medium heat and bring to the boil, stirring well all the time. Once the sauce is thickened, turn off the heat.
5. Put the drained vegetables in a casserole dish and pour the sauce over them. Top with grated cheese, put under the grill to brown or in the oven for 10 - 15 minutes.

Vegetarian

Cheesy Potatoes ★ ★

Vegetarian

This is a useful recipe. You can eat the potatoes on their own or serve them with bacon, sausages, or some grilled fish. If you are vegetarian, then serve with some green vegetables: broccoli or spring greens, green beans etc.. Cook the potatoes in a fairly large dish so that there is more surface area to brown on the top.

2 - 3 potatoes, cut into ¼" slices
1 x quantity of Quick Cheese Sauce (see page 23)
1 extra mug grated cheese
salt and pepper

1. Preheat oven to 180°C/gas reg 6.
2. Arrange the sliced potatoes in layers in the bottom of a small casserole dish.
3. Pour the cheese sauce over and season with salt and pepper.
4. Top with the grated cheese.
5. Bake in the oven for 30 - 35 minutes or until the potatoes are cooked and the cheese is browned. Test the potatoes with a fork. If they are not cooked turn the oven down and leave for another 10 minutes.
6. Serve with bacon, sausages or salad.

Cheese and Onion Rosti ★★

Serves 2   Preparation and cooking time 20 minutes

Vegetarian

This recipe makes a change to jacket potatoes. You can make Rosti with just potatoes, potatoes and onion, or potatoes and cheese.

2 potatoes
I onion
½ mug grated cheese
I tablespoon freeze dried basil
oil to cook
tomatoes and spring onions to garnish

1. Grate the potatoes and onion and mix with the cheese and the basil.
2. Divide into two and form 'cakes'.
3. Heat the oil in the frying pan and cook on a moderate heat for 5 minutes each side.
4. Serve with salad.

Spicy Vegetable Pasta Bake ★ ★

Serves 2   Preparation time 15 minutes, cooking time 25 minutes

Vegetarian

If you like hot and spicy vegetarian food, this is the dish for you. The vegetables can be varied. If you use things like potatoes and carrots, you will need to boil them before adding to the mixture.

2 mugs uncooked pasta
1 tin Campbell's condensed cream
of tomato soup, undiluted
1 tablespoon cooking oil, for frying
6 mushrooms, sliced
1 onion, chopped
2 courgettes, sliced

½ red or green pepper, sliced
1 red chilli, chopped finely
2 cloves garlic, finely chopped
1 teaspoon mixed herbs
2 teaspoons Worcestershire Sauce
1 mug grated cheese

1. Preheat oven to 200°C/gas reg 7
2. Cook the pasta (see page 12).
3. Fry the onions until soft.
4. Add the mushrooms, courgettes, peppers, herbs and chilli. Cook for 2 minutes.
5. Add the tomato soup, bring to the boil and then take off the heat. Add the Worcestershire sauce.
6. Drain the pasta and stir into the vegetable mixture.
7. Turn into a casserole dish and top with the grated cheese.
8. Cook for 25 minutes or until the cheese is browned.

Pasta and Cheese Bake ★★

Serves 1
Preparation time 10 minutes, cooking time 20 minutes

Vegetarian

This dish is a tasty variation on the old macaroni cheese, it is quick to make and inexpensive.

1 x quantity of Quick Cheese Sauce (see page 23)
¾ mug pasta
1 tomato
1 egg

1 teaspoon freeze dried chives
½ teaspoon mustard
1 packet of plain crisps
½ mug grated cheese

1. Make the cheese sauce and leave to cool a little.
2. Preheat oven to 180°C/gas reg 6.
3. Cook the pasta (see page 12).
4. Beat the egg in a mug, add the chives and the mustard and mix with the cheese sauce.
5. Drain the pasta and put into a small casserole dish or oven proof bowl. Cut the tomato into 8 and mix with the pasta. Pour the sauce over the top.
6. Crush the crisps in the bag and mix with the grated cheese. Sprinkle on the top of the pasta.
7. Bake for 20 minutes. The cheese and the crisps should be browned.
8. Serve with tomato, HP or Worcestershire Sauce.

Vegetarian

Potato Hash ★ ★

Serves 2   Preparation time 5 minutes, cooking time 30 minutes

Vegetarian

butter to fry
1 small onion, chopped
1 carrot, sliced
6 - 8 green beans
2 potatoes, cubed
2 teaspoons flour

vegetable stock cube + ½ mug water
8 oz tofu (can add flaked tuna, pieces of ham, corned beef etc.)
salt and pepper
1 teaspoon freeze dried parsley
2 teaspoons Worcestershire Sauce or HP sauce

1. Fry the onion, carrot, beans and potatoes. Cook for 5 - 7 minutes to brown the vegetables. Season well with salt and pepper.
2. Add the flour and cook for 1 minute.
3. Add the stock cube and ½ mug water, together with the Worcestershire sauce.
4. Bring to the boil and then simmer for 15 minutes until the vegetables are tender.
5. Add the tofu or ham, corned beef or tuna and cook for 5 minutes.
6. Add the parsley and season well.

Fish in Creamy Sauce **

Serves 1   Preparation time 15 - 20 minutes

This recipe is a little more pricy, but healthy and quite easy to do. You can, of course, substitute pasta or rice for the potatoes.

1 salmon steak	1 teaspoon freeze dried basil or parsley
½ - ⅓ cup pasta	oil to fry
a few green vegetables	salt and pepper
¼ cup double cream	potatoes, pasta or rice

1. Put potatoes on to boil. Add the green vegetables to the pan after 7 - 8 minutes, they will then be cooked at the same time. If you use pasta, add the green vegetables at the beginning, this means using only one pan!

2. Heat a little oil in a frying pan and cook the salmon steak. Use a high heat to seal each side first and then cook on a medium heat for approximately 10 minutes, depending on the size of the steak. If it is small and thin then it will only need 5 minutes.

3. Put the cream in a small pan and boil for about 1 minute, it will thicken slightly. Add the basil or parsley.

4. Drain the pasta/potatoes and beans, add a little butter. Serve with the fish and the sauce.

Tuna and Pasta Bake ★

Serves 2 - 3   Preparation time 5 - 10 minutes, cooking time 20 minutes

This is a classic, very easy dish to cook. It is inexpensive and you can reheat the leftovers successfully. You can use different condensed soups, celery or chicken, for example.

1 tin Campbell's condensed cream of mushroom soup
1 can of tuna steak, drained of oil or water.
2 mugs pasta
½ mug grated cheese
1 packet of crisps

1. Preheat the oven to 190°C/gas reg 7.
2. Cook the pasta (see page 12).
3. Drain and place back in the saucepan. Add the tuna and condensed soup (do not dilute the soup). Mix well.
4. Transfer to a casserole dish.
5. Crush the crisps in the bag, mix with the grated cheese and sprinkle on top of the mixture in the casserole dish.
6. Cook for 20 minutes until the cheese and crisps are browned.

Tuna and Rice ★

Serves 2
Cooking and preparation time 10 - 15 minutes

This recipe is extremely easy. You can use celery or chicken soup for variety and cook egg fried rice to accompany the dish (see page 13).

1 tin Campbell's condensed cream of mushroom soup
1 tin tuna steak, drained of oil or water
1 mug rice
2 mugs water
salt and pepper

1. Put rice on to cook (see page 13).
2. Place the soup in the pan and heat, do not dilute as the tin suggests. Bring to the boil.
3. Add the tuna and break up a little. Heat for 1 - 2 minutes. Season well with pepper.
4. Serve with the rice and some green vegetables, peas or beans. Season well.

Fish

fishy Pasta Bake ★ ★ ★

Serves 2
Preparation time 20 minutes, cooking time 20 minutes

You can use different kinds of fish in this recipe: salmon, haddock, smoked haddock, trout. If you find fish on offer at the supermarket, buy it and freeze ready to make dishes like this.

2 - 3 pieces of cod fillet (you can buy packets of frozen fillets)
1 small stem broccoli, broken into 'small trees'
2 spring onions, chopped
1 mug milk
½ mug frozen peas
1 teaspoon freeze dried parsley

1 mug pasta
2 teaspoon cornflour
salt and pepper
½ mug grated cheese for the top

1.   Preheat oven to 180°C/gas reg 6.
2.   Cook the pasta, broccoli and peas in the same pan for approximately 5 minutes, depending on the pasta you use.
3.   Place the fish and the milk in a frying pan and cook gently for 4 - 5 minutes. Remove the fish.
4.   Mix the cornflower with a little milk and add to the hot milk in the pan, it should thicken.
5.   Break up the fish gently and add to the thickened milk.
6.   Drain the pasta and vegetables well. Add to the fish mixture. Add the chopped spring onions. Season with salt and pepper and stir gently.
7.   Pour into a casserole dish and top with the grated cheese. Cook for 20 minutes. The cheese should be browned.

Fishy Rice ★★

Serves 1   Preparation and cooking time 15 minutes

This recipe is based on the old Kedgeree dish. It is quite easy to do and makes a refreshing change from any fast food you may buy.

½ mug rice cooked with a pilau rice cube (see page 13)

1 piece smoked haddock	1 teaspoon curry paste
1 tablespoon milk	1 - 2 mushrooms, sliced
1 hard-boiled egg (see page 20)	½ teaspoon lemon juice
1 onion, chopped	1 teaspoon freeze dried parsley or basil

1. Boil egg and peel the shell off, cut into 4.
2. Cook mushrooms and onion in a little butter in the frying pan, add the curry paste and mix. Take out of pan and leave to one side.
3. Put fish and milk in the frying pan and cook gently for 3 - 4 minutes, the fish should flake away from the skin when it is done.
4. Remove the fish skin from the pan and add the eggs, rice, mushrooms, lemon juice and parsley. Mix together and heat for 1 minute.
5. Can be eaten either hot or cold.

Fish

Spicy Prawns ★ ★

Serves 2   Preparation time 15 minutes

Although prawns are fairly pricy, with this recipe you can make a few prawns go a long way. It is not recommended that you reheat prawns, so if you make enough for 2 people, it is best to share it with a flatmate.

1 tablespoon oil to fry	200g pack of peeled prawns
1 clove garlic, chopped very finely	1 teaspoon sugar
½ onion, chopped finely	½ teaspoon curry paste
1 x 7 oz/200g tin of chopped tomatoes	¼ teaspoon freeze dried basil
1 dessertspoon tomato puree	salt and pepper

1. Fry the onion and garlic in the oil until the onions begin to brown.
2. Add the tinned tomatoes, tomato puree, sugar and curry paste and bring to the boil. Let the mixture cook for 2 - 3 minutes.
3. Add the prawns, basil and salt and pepper. Cook for 2 - 3 minutes keeping the heat quite high. If the tomato mixture is very hot, and you keep the heat under the pan quite high, this will be sufficient to cook the prawns. If you cook them for too long, they will become rubbery. Keep prawns in the fridge. Eat within one day.
4. Serve with rice.

Salmon Pasta ★★

Serves 1   Preparation time 15 minutes

You will only need a small piece of salmon for the dish, so it will not prove too expensive. It makes a scrumptious meal if you are looking for something a little different.

3 spring onions, chopped
1 small piece of salmon
½ x 200 ml pot of double cream
1 teaspoon freeze dried chives

2 small bunches of tagliatelle pasta
salt and pepper
olive oil to fry

1. Cook the pasta, it should only take about 3 - 4 minutes to cook (See page 12). Leave to drain.
2. Fry the salmon in a little olive oil, if you have a small piece it should only take 2 - 3 minutes each side. Add the spring onions to the pan towards the end of the cooking time and allow them to brown a little.
3. Remove the pan from the heat and gently break up the salmon. Add the cream and the chives and return to the heat. As soon as the cream begins to bubble, add the pasta and stir everything together. Allow the pasta to heat through, this should take 1 minute maximum.
4. Serve on a plate and season well with salt and pepper. Enjoy!

fisherman's Pie ★ ★ ★

Serves 2

Preparation time 20 minutes, cooking time 20 minutes

This dish is slightly more complicated, but worth the extra effort. Fish does not reheat too well, so this one is best shared.

2 pieces cod or haddock fillet (defrost if frozen)
2 hard boiled eggs, each cut into 4 (see page 20)

1 mug milk	½ mug grated cheese
2 teaspoons cornflour	1 teaspoon freeze dried parsley or basil
5 medium potatoes, washed and diced	1 teaspoon butter
salt and pepper	

1. Preheat the oven to 200°C/gas reg 7.
2. Place the milk and fish in the frying pan and simmer gently for approximately 5 minutes, or until the fish turns white.
3. Mix the cornflour with a little milk to make a paste and add to the pan. Stir well into the milk, the sauce will thicken. Season with salt and pepper and gently break up the fish.
4. Add the hard boiled egg and the herbs. Mix gently and pour into a casserole dish.
5. Boil the diced potatoes for 8 - 10 minutes, drain off the water, add the butter and stir gently.
6. Place the potatoes on the top of the fish mixture and top with the grated cheese.
7. Cook for 20 minutes, the top should be browned.
8. Serve with green vegetables or salad.

Bacon and Egg Pasta ★★

Serves 2   Preparation time 15 minutes

Makes a meal in itself with green salad or you can use it at barbecues or parties.

4 rashers bacon
2 hard-boiled eggs
1 mug pasta
3 spring onions
3 mushrooms, sliced
2 tablespoons mayonnaise
1 tablespoon olive oil, for frying
salt and pepper

1. Cook the pasta and the eggs in the same pan. Boil the water and add the eggs first and then the pasta a few minutes later, so that it does not overcook: i.e. eggs for 10 minutes, then pasta and eggs for a further 5 minutes.
2. Fry the bacon until crisp and the mushrooms until browned. Cut the bacon into bite- size pieces.
3. Chop the spring onions.
4. Mix the oil and mayonnaise together.
5. Drain the pasta and take the shells off the eggs. Cut the eggs into four.
6. Mix everything together and serve with a little green salad.

Salami Salad ★★

Serves 2   Preparation time 15 minutes

This makes a lovely, refreshing summer meal. Salami is inexpensive, but needs the right accompaniments to compliment its strong taste.

rocket or lettuce
1 tablespoon olive oil
8 slices salami
3 mushrooms, sliced
½ onion, chopped finely
¼ red pepper, chopped
2 tomatoes
3" piece of cucumber

Dressing - you can make your own
or use a ready-made vinaigrette dressing:
juice of ½ lemon
3 tablespoons olive oil
1 clove garlic, chopped very finely
1 tablespoon white wine vinegar
1 tablespoon sugar

1. Fry the mushrooms, onion and pepper until browned. Leave to cool.
2. Wash lettuce or rocket and spread over the plate.
3. Chop tomatoes and cucumber. Add the salami, mushrooms, onion and pepper and arrange them on top of the rocket or lettuce.
4. Mix the dressing ingredients together and pour over the salad.
5. Eat straight away as the dressing will make the rocket and lettuce wilt and go brown.

Cold Chicken and Nut Salad *

Serves 1   Preparation time 15 minutes

You can use left-over chicken for this recipe. If you like the combination of sweet and savoury, you will like this dish. There is also a contrast of textures; you can add other things to it such as spring onions, orange segments, peppers, mushrooms or cucumber.

cooked chicken - either one chicken breast or 2 - 3 small chicken fillets
1 eating apple, Granny Smith or Golden Delicious
6 - 8 walnuts or pecans or ¼ mug cashews
¼ mug raisins
2 tablespoons mayonnaise
2 celery sticks

2 tablespoons creme frais
1 teaspoon freeze dried chives
green salad to serve

1. Cut the chicken into bite-sized pieces.
2. Chop the celery into ½" pieces.
3. Cut the apple into small pieces, leaving the skin on.
4. Cut the walnuts or pecans in half, add the cashews whole.
5. Mix the mayonnaise and creme frais with the chives and the raisins.
6. Mix everything together and serve with green salad.

Cold Chicken Salad ★

Serves 2
Preparation and cooking time 10 - 15 minutes

Any leftovers can be used in sandwiches the next day.

½ x 500g chicken mince or
2 chicken breasts cut into small pieces
1 red onion, chopped
1 teaspoon soy sauce
juice of ½ lime
1 clove garlic, finely chopped

1 teaspoon curry paste
2 teaspoons brown sugar
1 teaspoon freeze dried coriander
a little oil to fry
salt and pepper

1. Fry the onion in the oil until soft.
2. Add the mince and fry until the meat is no longer pink.
3. Add the rest of the ingredients. Cook for 2 minutes and leave to cool.
4. Serve with salad.

Couscous Salad ★

Serves 1   Preparation time 10 minutes

You need to add plenty of tasty things to couscous plus some kind of dressing or sauce. It is very easy to prepare as all you have to do is add hot water to couscous.

½ mug couscous
1 mug boiling water
1 tomato
2 spring onions
1" cucumber, cut into cubes
1 teaspoon olive oil
juice of ½ lemon
1 clove garlic, finely chopped
1 teaspoon freeze dried chives
¼ red or green pepper, chopped coarsely
1 tablespoon salad dressing or oil
1 teaspoon butter to fry

Optional additions:
2 slices ham, cut into bite-sized pieces
3 - 4 slices salami, cut into pieces
prawns
smoked mackerel or tuna, broken into pieces

1. Put the couscous in a bowl and add the boiling water. Leave to stand for about 4 minutes. All the water should have been absorbed into the couscous, if not, drain off the excess. Add 1 teaspoon butter and cook in a small pan on a medium heat for 1 minute. Leave to cool.
2. Chop the tomato, spring onion and pepper into small pieces.
3. Mix the salad dressing or oil, lemon, garlic and chives together.
4. Mix all the ingredients together, including the optional additions, and serve with a green salad.

Rice Salad ★★

Serves 4
Preparation time 15 minutes

This is an ideal accompaniment to barbecues, or can be eaten with cold meats, baked potatoes, potato wedges or green salads. Along with the basic ingredients in this recipe you could also add peppers, cucumber, gherkins, celery or raisins.

1 mug rice
1 pilau rice cube or 1 teaspoon pilau rice seasoning
2 apples, Golden Delicious or Granny Smith
3 - 4 spring onions
½ tin sweetcorn
juice of ½ lemon
2 tablespoons olive oil
1 teaspoon freeze dried herbs

Vegetarian

1. Cook the rice with the pilau rice cube (see page 13).
2. Chop the apple into small pieces.
3. Mix oil, lemon juice and chives together.
4. Chop spring onions and mix all the ingredients together, including the sweetcorn.

Pasta Salad ★

Serves 4 if eaten with other things.

Preparation time 15 minutes

Vegetarian

Good for barbecues or with cold meats and other salads.

1 mug pasta
½ red onion, finely chopped
3 tablespoons mayo
1 red pepper, chopped
2 teaspoons freeze dried basil or chives
2 sticks celery, finely sliced
salt and pepper

1. Cook the pasta (see page 12). Drain well and allow to cool a little.
2. Prepare the other ingredients and mix them all together with the pasta.
3. Season well.

Bean Salad ★

Serves 4 if accompanying a meal.   Preparation time 10 minutes

Vegetarian

Great to eat with barbecues, sausages, beefburgers, bobotie and other salads. If you are vegetarian you can eat this as a main dish.

2 x 14 oz/400g tins of beans, flageolet, pinto, cannellini or haricot
1 pepper, chopped
½ red onion or 3 spring onions, chopped finely
2 tablespoons of olive oil
1 teaspoon freeze dried basil or chives
½ teaspoon curry paste
1 teaspoon sugar
salt and pepper

1. Open the beans and wash well in a colander. Leave to drain.
2. Chop the pepper and the onions and mix with the beans.
3. Mix together the olive oil, curry paste, chives and sugar and add to the bean mixture. Stir and season well with salt and pepper.

This is just a basic recipe. You can add other things to it such as apples cut into small pieces, avocado, chopped fresh tomatoes. You can vary the beans, but it is best to mix 2 varieties. Always take care to rinse the beans well as some of the soaking juices are not good for you.

Salads

Tuna Salad ★

Serves 2   Preparation time 10 - 15 minutes

This salad is great with barbecues or with cold meats, sausages etc. Again you can add other ingredients: cucumber, tomatoes or some curry paste to spice it up a little.

1 mug pasta
3 tablespoons mayonnaise or seafood dressing (Thousand Island)
½ tin tuna, drained of oil
1 mug frozen peas
4 - 5 spring onions
1 red pepper
1 teaspoon freeze dried chives
salt and pepper

1. Cook pasta and peas in the same pan. Drain and cool.
2. Chop onions and pepper.
3. Flake the tuna, season with salt and pepper, and mix all the ingredients together.
4. Serve with lettuce and tomatoes.

Potato Salad ★ ★

Serves 2
Preparation time 15 minutes

Serve with cold meats and green salad. Ideal with barbecue food. You can add other things to this salad: peppers, cucumber, tomatoes, peas for example.

2 medium sized potatoes
4 - 5 spring onions
1 teaspoon freeze dried chives
1 teaspoon freeze dried mint
2 tablespoons creme frais
3 dessertspoons mayonnaise

Vegetarian

1. Cut the potatoes into cubes and boil for 10 minutes.
2. Drain and leave to cool.
3. Mix the mayonnaise and creme frais together. Add chives and mint.
4. Chop the onions and mix everything together.

Salsa Salad ★★

Serves 2   Preparation time 20 minutes

6 large tomatoes
lettuce
2 hard-boiled eggs
3 spring onions, chopped
I clove garlic, chopped finely
2 tablespoon olive oil

juice of ½ a lemon
I teaspoon freeze dried chives
2 medium potatoes or 8 small new potatoes
4 rashers of unsmoked bacon
salt and pepper

1. Boil the eggs, see page 20. When cooked, run them under cold water, this stops the yolk becoming discoloured. Peel off the shells and cut each one into 4 pieces.
2. If you are using old potatoes, wash and cut them into I" dice. If you are using new potatoes, cut each one in ½. Boil them for 10 - 15 minutes until they are cooked. Drain and leave to cool.
3. Make the salsa using 3 of the tomatoes. Chop them into quite small pieces. Put in a bowl and add the chopped spring onions, garlic, chives, lemon juice and olive oil. Season with salt and pepper and mix well.
4. Fry or grill the bacon until it is crisp, then cut into bite-size pieces.
5. Cut the remaining tomatoes into ¼'s.
6. Wash and drain the lettuce and arrange on the two plates. Arrange the tomatoes, potatoes, bacon and eggs on the top. Pour the salsa over the top and serve.

Hot Potato Salad ★ ★

Serves 2
Preparation time 15 minutes

This can be a meal in itself if served with green salad, or as an accompaniment to a barbecue.
It can be eaten hot or cold.

4 rashers of bacon
4 - 5 mushrooms
3 potatoes
4 - 5 spring onions
oil for frying

1 teaspoon freeze dried parsley
3 tablespoons olive oil
1 teaspoon mustard
1 tablespoon white wine vinegar

1. Cut the potatoes into medium sized chunks, boil for 10 minutes and drain.
2. Slice mushrooms and fry in a little oil until browned.
3. Fry bacon until brown and then cut into small pieces.
4. Mix the oil, mustard and white wine vinegar together in a mug.
5. Mix all the other ingredients together, taking care not to break the potatoes up too much.
Pour the dressing over the top and stir a little.

Salads

Quick Cheese Cake ★★★

Serves 4   Preparation time 15 – 20 minutes.   Refrigeration time 4 hours.

250g packet of digestive biscuits
¼ x 500g pack of butter
250g packet of cream cheese
10 fl oz/ ½ pint tub of double cream

2 tablespoons white sugar
Rind and juice of a lemon
Fruit to decorate, e.g. oranges or strawberries

1. Put the digestive biscuits into a polythene bag and crush them with a rolling pin, milk bottle or tin of beans. There should be no lumps left, just crumbs!
2. Melt the butter in a saucepan and add the crushed biscuit. Mix well.
3. Press the biscuit mixture into the bottom of a 20cm cake tin. If you do not have a cake tin, use a small casserole dish.
4. Beat the cream and sugar together with a whisk until the cream thickens. Don't keep beating once it has thickened or it will turn to butter.
5. Gently fold in the cream cheese, grated lemon rind and juice. The lemon juice is essential as it helps the cream to set. Pour on to the top of the biscuit mixture and gently spread out.
6. Leave in the fridge for 4 hours to set.
7. Decorate the top with fruit.

In order to get the cheesecake out of the tin, you will need to use a cake tin with a loose bottom. Once the cheesecake has set, loosen the side with a knife and place the loose bottomed tin on a jam jar or tin and push the sides down. If you do not have an appropriate tin, you can use a casserole dish, but you will have to serve the cheesecake from it. Don't try to get it out all in one piece!

Serves 4   Preparation time 5 minutes

This is a very quick and easy way of producing a dessert if you have friends around for a meal. Keep the ingredients in your store cupboard and the ice cream in your freezer drawer! You can add things on top of the chocolate sauce, such as chopped nuts, 100's and 1000's, Smarties, broken up Flakes, small sweets etc.

¼ x 500g pack butter
3 heaped tablespoons drinking chocolate
4 heaped tablespoons sugar (brown or white)
2 tablespoons milk
ice cream

1. Place the butter, sugar and chocolate in a saucepan. Heat, stir well, and allow to boil for 1 minute.
2. Add the milk, carefully, as it may spit at you! Boil for another 1 minute, stirring all the time. It should be smooth and thick by now.
3. Allow to cool slightly before serving on top of the ice cream. You will need to leave the sauce to cool longer if you are using glass dishes, as the contrasts in temperature between the sauce and the ice cream may break thinner glass.

Boozy Chocolate Trifle ★ ★

Serves 4 - 6
Preparation time 10 minutes, refrigeration time 2 - 3 hours

Very easy to make and will impress your friends when you have them around for a meal.
Raspberries are the best fruit to use, but you could also use apricots or pineapple. You will
need to chop larger fruits up a little.

1 chocolate Swiss roll
1 x 14 oz/400g tin raspberries
¼ mug sherry or brandy or Tia Maria or Cointreau,
10 fl oz/ ½ pint tub of double cream
2 tablespoon sugar
1 Cadbury's flake

1. Slice the Swiss roll into 1" pieces and arrange around the bottom of a dish. A glass
dish is preferable, but a casserole dish will work just as well.
2. Pour the liquor evenly over the cake.
3. Put the raspberries and ½ the juice from the tin over the cake.
4. Whip the cream and sugar with a whisk until thickened, pour on the top.
5. Decorate the top with the broken up flake. Leave in the fridge for 2 - 3 hours until set.

Fruit Salad ★

Fruit salad is extremely easy to make. It will not last more than one day, as the fruits will begin to go brown. If you just have two or three fruits, you can liven them up by making them into a salad. You can use a variety of fruits which could include those listed below.

apples
pears
oranges
bananas
seedless grapes
strawberries
kiwi fruits
pineapple
peaches
nectarines
raspberries

For the juice
You can use either pure apple or orange fruit juice.
If you prefer a more tangy fruit salad, try the following:
1 lemon
1 orange
1 tablespoon sugar
¼ mug water

1. To make the juice, grate the rind of the lemon and the orange and squeeze the juices from both fruits. Add the sugar and the water. Leave for the sugar to dissolve.
2. Cut the fruit into small pieces and mix together. If you use raspberries and strawberries, add them at the end or they will break up in the mix and everything will be pink!
3. Serve with whipped cream.

Banana Split ★

Serves 1   Preparation time 5 minutes

Very easy dessert, quick to make and a good one when you have others around for a meal.

1 banana
2 scoops of ice cream
chocolate sauce, see page 113
1 Cadbury's flake

1. Make chocolate sauce, see page 113.
2. Slice banana in half lengthways and arrange on the plate or dish.
3. Place 2 scoops of ice cream on the plate, pour over the chocolate sauce and sprinkle the broken up flake over the top.

Other ideas for easy ice cream type deserts:

Sundaes made from layers of different flavours of ice cream, mixed with fresh or tinned fruit, chocolate or jam sponge rolls. You can decorate them with many varieties of sweets e.g. M&M's, Maltesers, grated chocolate, cut up Mars bars, Snickers bars, nuts etc.. Just go to the chocolate and sweet counter at the supermarket and the world is your oyster!!

Cakes & Desserts

fried Bananas ★

Serves 1   Preparation time 5 minutes

This is a really quick, easy and impressive dessert to make for a special meal or when friends come around.

1 banana
1 teaspoon butter
¼ teaspoon cinnamon
2 teaspoons sugar
double cream, creme frais, or yogurt to serve

1. Slice the banana in half lengthways and then cut each piece in half.
2. Melt the butter in the frying pan, add the sugar and cinnamon. Cook for 1 minute on medium heat. The mixture should be bubbling a little.
3. Add the bananas to the pan and cook for a further minute on medium heat. The butter and sugar should be forming a fudgy sauce.
4. Arrange the banana on a plate. Pour the sauce over the banana and add a good serving of cream, creme frais or yogurt. You can get Greek yogurt with honey which works very well with the bananas.

You can cook maybe 3 bananas at a time in a frying pan. If you have more people, you will need to wash the pan between each batch or the sauce will not work.

Chocolate Chip Cookies ★ ★

Makes 16   Preparation time 15 minutes, cooking time 10 - 12 minutes

These cookies are delicious, crunchy on the outside and a bit gooey on the inside. Don't skimp on the butter and use margarine, it won't taste nearly as good!

½ x 250g packet of butter (make sure it has been out of the fridge for a while).
1 mug of soft brown sugar
1 large egg
1 teaspoon of vanilla extract
1½ mugs self raising flour
1 x 100g packet of chocolate chips, ½ milk and ½ white works well.

1. Preheat the oven to 180°C/gas reg 6. Grease 2 baking trays. If you only have one tray, you can cook them in two batches. The mixture will be OK to leave ½, while the other ½ cooks.
2. Mix the butter and sugar together and beat well. Add the egg and the vanilla extract. Beat well.
3. Add the chocolate chips and mix, then add the flour and mix well. The cookie dough will be quite stiff. Tip onto a floured surface and squash into a long sausage. Do not knead the dough, in fact, handle it as little as possible. Cut into 16 and roll each portion into a ball and then squash so it is about ½" thick and approximately 2½" across. Place on the baking tray.
4. Put in the oven and bake for 10 - 12 minutes. The cookies do not need to brown, just be crisp on the outside. Leave to cool for a few minutes. The cookies should be a little soft on the inside.
5. If you want to make double Chocolate Chip Cookies, then replace 2 tablespoons of the flour with 2 tablespoons of drinking chocolate.

Rice Krispie Cakes ★

Makes 12

Preparation time 10 minutes, cooling time 15 minutes

These are scrummy! You can find other recipes for these which involve measuring syrup etc., but this one is really easy, all you need are Mars bars and butter and Rice Krispies!

3 normal size Mars bars
¼ x 250g block of butter
2 mugs of Rice Krispies
12 paper cake cases

1. Cut the Mars bars up into chunks.
2. Melt the butter slowly in a large pan and then add the chopped up Mars bars. Cook gently over a low heat, stirring frequently. The Mars bars will melt and form a thick creamy mixture.
3. Add the Rice Krispies and stir quickly.
4. Divide the mixture into the 12 cake cases (use two spoons as the mixture will be quite hot).
5. It is best if you allow them to cool for 15 minutes, but one or two may disappear before then! If they last long enough you can put them in the fridge.

Cakes and Desserts

Gingerbread Men ★ ★ ★ ★

Makes about 12   Preparation time 40 minutes + 1 hour in the fridge, cooking time 8 mins

These are fiddly to make but fun. You do NOT need a gingerbread man cutter, neither do you need to be an art student. Just draw your own gingerbread family on some paper, cut them out and then, when you have rolled out the dough, cut around them with a pointed knife.

2 ½ mugs of self raising flour
2 teaspoons ground ginger
100g or ⅖ x 250g block of butter
1 egg
2 tablespoons golden syrup
½ mug sugar

icing
⅔ mug icing sugar
2 tablespoons water

1. Grease a baking tray with some butter.
2. Put the butter and sugar in a bowl and beat together with a wooden spoon.
3. Add the egg and beat well. Add the golden syrup and beat again until smooth.
4. Add the flour and ground ginger, mix together with a metal spoon. The mixture will be quite stiff. Turn out onto a floured surface and knead together. Cover with cling film and leave in the fridge for an hour.
5. Put the oven on to heat at 180°C/gas reg 6.
6. Place the dough on a floured surface and roll out, if you do not have a rolling pin use a glass bottle. The dough should be about ¼" thick. Place the ginger people templates on the dough and cut out with a pointed knife. Gather together the spare pieces and squash together, re-roll and cut out some more men. Do not re-roll again as the biscuits will be really hard.
7. Place the men on the baking tray, you can add eyes and mouths now using currants or raisins, or you can decorate later, see no. 8. Cook for 8 minutes. If you only have one tray the dough is fine to wait until each batch is cooked.
8. Take off the tray and leave to cool. Decorate if you wish. To make the icing simply mix the icing sugar and water together. If you do not have an icing bag make one out of greaseproof paper. Take a square piece of greaseproof paper and make a cone, sellotape together, put the icing inside and then snip off the tip of the cone. Screw the top of the cone around and squeeze, the icing should come out of the hole. Make sure the top end is screwed tight or the icing will come out of the wrong end! Decorate the biscuits however you want.

Cakes & Desserts

Astri's Apple Cake ★ ★

Makes about 16   Preparation time 20 minutes, cooking time 25 minutes

I have used this recipe for many years. It was passed on to me by a Norwegian friend called Astri. These cakes can also be used as a dessert if you serve them with cream or custard.

150g or ⅗ x 250g block butter
¾ mug sugar
3 eggs
1 ½ mugs self raising flour
3 tablespoons cold water
2 drops of vanilla essence (optional)
2 medium sized apples (cooking apples are best but you can use eating apples)

Topping
¼ mug sugar
1 teaspoon cinnamon

1. Put the oven on to heat 180°C/gas reg 6. Grease a baking tray, if you have greaseproof paper put a piece in the bottom of the tray. Put the sugar and cinnamon in a mug and mix.
2. Peel the apples, cut into ¼'s, take out the core and then slice each ¼ lengthways again 3 or 4 times. Set aside.
3. Cream the butter and sugar together with a wooden spoon. When the mixture is quite soft, it should also lighten in colour, add the eggs and beat well. Add the vanilla essence.
4. Fold in the flour with a metal spoon. Do not beat. Add the water and stir gently. The mixture should still be quite stiff.
5. Turn into the baking tray and spread out evenly. Push the apple slices into the mix, distributing them as evenly as possible. Sprinkle the sugar and cinnamon evenly over the top.
6. Bake in the preheated oven for 25 minutes. The top should be nicely brown.
7. Leave to cool and cut into squares.

Squidgy Chocolate Pudding ★ ★

Serves 4 Preparation time 15 minutes, cooking time 30 minutes

This is a fun dessert to make and eat with friends. You can serve it with cream, ice cream, creme frais or custard! It should have a crisp outside and a runny inside. It is best served hot.

½ x 250g block of butter
¾ mug soft brown sugar
4 eggs, beaten
1 x 200g block of dark cooking chocolate
1 teaspoon vanilla extract
½ mug self raising flour

1. Put the oven on at 180°C/gas reg 6. Grease a dish, it should be about 7" x 9" and approximately 2" deep. If you don't have one, use your casserole dish.
2. Mix the butter and sugar together and beat well with a wooden spoon. Add the eggs and beat well.
3. Melt the chocolate gently in a pan over a low heat. Once it is all melted, add to the sugar and butter and egg mixture along with the vanilla extract. Mix well.
4. Add the flour and stir in with a metal spoon. Pour into the greased dish and cook for 30 minutes. The outside will be crisp and the inside runny. Serve hot.

Muffins ★ ★

Makes 24   Preparation time 10 minutes, cooking time 20 minutes

Muffins are very easy and inexpensive to make. The flavourings can be varied according to what you may have in the cupboards.

Basic recipe
3 mugs self raising flour
1 mug of brown sugar,
you can use white.
2 eggs, slightly beaten
1½ mugs milk
¾ mug vegetable oil

Variations
Chocolate chip muffins - add two 100g packets of chocolate chips. Two different varieties work well; for example, white and milk or plain chocolate. If you want double choc chip muffins, instead of the 3 mugs of flour, use 2⅔ flour and ⅓ mug drinking chocolate.

Raspberry or blueberry muffins - take a 14 oz tin of the fruit, drain the liquid from the fruit and add to the basic mixture.

Apple cinnamon muffins - add 1 mug of finely chopped apple to the mixture, with 2 teaspoons ground cinnamon.

Banana and nuts - add 1 mug of mashed, ripe banana plus 1 mug of chopped nuts, cashews, Brazils, pecans or walnuts.

Method
1. Preheat oven to 180°C/gas reg 6.
2. Mix all the dry ingredients together, then add the 'wet ones'. They will be a bit lumpy and quite 'wet'.
3. If you do not have the individual cake tins, use your flat baking tray and arrange as many cake papers as you can on the tray. If you use them double, they will hold their shape better. If you only have one baking tray, the mixture will be OK if you leave it in the bowl whilst the first batch cooks. Bake in the oven for 20 minutes.

Flap Jacks ★

Makes about 18
Preparation time 5 minutes, cooking time 20 minutes

Flap Jacks are so easy to cook and make good comfort food when you are working hard or doing revision. The oats provide good fibre content to your diet!

2 mugs rolled oats
½ mug soft brown sugar
½ x 250g block of butter
3 rounded tablespoons golden syrup

1. Preheat the oven to 170°C/gas reg 4.
2. Melt the butter and the syrup very gently over a low heat. Use a large pan.
3. Add the sugar and stir well for 2 minutes. Do not allow it to boil.
4. Add the oats and mix well.
5. Pour into a greased flat baking tray and bake in the oven for 20 - 25 minutes.
6. Leave to cool for about 10 minutes. While the mixture is still warm, and in the baking tray, cut into squares. Should make about 18. Leave in the tin to cool and set.

Scones ★ ★

Makes 12 Preparation time 10 minutes, cooking time 15 minutes

Scones are quite easy to make and inexpensive. They are, of course, delicious with jam and cream, but you can make them with cheese and, depending on your taste, also eat them with jam, but not the cream! They are a fun Sunday afternoon snack.

Basic plain scones
2 mugs of self raising flour
¼ teaspoon salt
½ x 250g block of butter
I egg
+ milk to make ⅔ of a mug

Savoury
Add ¾ mug of grated cheese before you add the liquid.

Sweet
Add ⅓ mug of sugar.
If you want, you can also add ½ mug of raisins.

1. Preheat the oven to 180°C/gas reg 6. Grease a flat baking tray.
2. Place flour and salt in a mixing bowl; use a casserole dish if you do not have a mixing bowl. Chop the butter into small pieces, add to the flour and rub in with your fingers. Try not to work it too much or for too long.
3. If you are making plain scones, go to No. 4. If you are making either of the variations, add the extra ingredients in now and stir.
4. Break the egg into a mug and beat with a fork, add the milk to make up to ⅔ of a mug of liquid in total.
5. Add to the mixture and mix well with a knife. The mixture should be soft, but not sticky.
6. Turn out on to a floured surface and gently squash the mixture so it is flat and about 2" thick. Do not knead at this point; the less you handle the mixture the better. Use round cutters if you have them, but if not, squash the mixture into a neat square shape and cut square scones, as in the photograph.
7. Place them on the tray with a little space between them for them to rise and spread a little. Brush the top of the scones with a little milk. Use your fingers if you do not have a brush.
8. Place in the oven for 15 - 20 minutes. They should rise a little and be brown on the top. If they spread into one another a little, don't worry, allow them to cool and you will be able to cut them apart.

Cakes & Desserts

Nicole's Nutty Brownies ★ ★ ★

Makes about 15   Preparation time 15 minutes, cooking time 30 minutes

These are dedicated to Nicole (now married to Ben) as they are her favourite food to cook! They are truly scrummy. Brownies are meant to be soggy on the inside and crisp on the outside, so don't think they are not cooked, or that you have failed when you sample their delicious soggy bit!

100g pack of chopped mixed nuts
½ x 200g block of dark cooking chocolate
just under ½ x 250g block of butter
3 large eggs, beaten
I mug of granulated sugar
½ mug self raising flour

1. Heat the oven to 160°C/gas reg 4.
2. Grease a flat baking tray and line with greaseproof paper.
3. Put the butter and chocolate in a pan and heat gently over a low heat until melted.
4. Put all the dry ingredients into a bowl and mix.
5. Stir in the beaten eggs and then the chocolate and butter.
6. Pour into the baking tray and cook for 30 minutes. The brownies should be springy in the centre when you press lightly with your fingers.
7. Leave to cool. The brownies will rise in the oven and then go down when you take them out. Cut into squares.

Snickerdoodles ★★

Makes 24
Preparation time 15 minutes, cooking time 12 minutes

1⅔ mugs self raising flour
½ teaspoon nutmeg
½ x 250g block of butter
½ mug sugar

1 egg, beaten
1 teaspoon vanilla extract
1 tablespoon cinnamon
2 tablespoons sugar

1. Preheat the oven to 160°C/gas reg 4. Grease a flat baking tray.
2. Mix the butter and the ½ mug of sugar together and beat with a wooden spoon. Add the beaten egg and vanilla and beat well.
3. Mix in the flour and the nutmeg until the mixture is smooth.
4. Place the 2 tablespoons of sugar and the cinnamon on a plate and mix together.
5. Turn the cookie mixture out onto a surface and squash together. Make into a long sausage, handling as little as possible. Cut into 24. Take each piece and make into a small ball, roll this in the sugar and cinnamon, squash slightly and place on the baking tray.
6. Bake for 12 minutes. The snickerdoodles should be slightly browned.

Cakes & Desserts

Chocolate Cake ★★

Preparation time 10 - 15 minutes, cooking time 25 - 30 minutes

If you are a chocoholic, this is an excellent recipe. You do not need a food processor. A cake tin is the best, but you can cook it in a casserole dish!

⅓ x 500g tub of soft margarine or butter
¾ mug sugar
3 eggs
1 mug self raising flour
3 tablespoons drinking chocolate

small carton of cream for the filling
bar of Dairy Milk for the topping
1 Flake for the topping
1 tablespoon water if required

1. Preheat the oven to 170°C/gas reg 5.
2. Grease the cake tins well. If you have two 8" round tins they are the best, but you could use a casserole dish. If you cut a round of greaseproof paper and put in the bottom of the cake tins or dish, this will help the cake to come out after cooking.
3. Put the butter and sugar in a bowl and beat well with a wooden spoon.
4. Add the eggs, one at a time, and beat well. The mixture should go quite pale.
5. Add the flour and the drinking chocolate, fold in gently with a metal spoon. Do not beat the cake mixture at this stage. If the eggs you used were small and the mixture is very stiff, add one tablespoon of water.

6. Pour the mixture into the tin and smooth out the top. Place in the oven for 25 - 30 minutes. When the cake is done, you should be able to gently press it in the centre and it will not leave an indentation, but rather 'bounce' back a little.
7. Leave the cake to cool. If you have used a single tin or dish, cut the cake in half, horizontally.
8. Put one half of the cake on a plate and spread with fresh whipped cream. Put the other half of the cake on top. Melt a bar of Dairy Milk and spread it over the top of the cake. Alternatively, you could make a quantity of chocolate sauce (see page 113), boil it well so it goes thick, leave to cool and then pour over the top of the cake. You can sprinkle a broken up Flake on the top in order to make the whole thing completely naughty!

Cakes and desserts

Scotch Pancakes ★

Preparation and cooking time 15 minutes

Scotch pancakes are really easy and inexpensive to make. You will usually have the ingredients in your cupboards, if not, check to see if someone else has! They are great to make on a Sunday afternoon, to eat whilst watching the TV or when friends drop in. Mixture makes approximately 16 small pancakes.

1 mug self raising flour
¼ mug brown sugar, can use white
2 eggs
¼ mug water
white flora or oil to fry

1. Put the eggs, sugar and flour in a bowl and beat with a wooden spoon.
2. Add the water and beat well, the mixture is quite thick.
3. Heat a small amount of oil in the frying pan until it is quite hot.
4. Put 4 separate dessert spoonfuls of the mixture in the hot pan and leave to cook for 1 minute. The mixture will rise slightly. Turn the pancakes over and cook on the other side for another minute The pancakes will rise a little more.
5. Take out of the pan and eat immediately with butter and jam, maple syrup, ice cream etc..

Cakes and desserts

Fondues ★★

Fondues are great fun. If you don't have a fondue set, find someone who does and borrow it.
If you plan ahead, you may find there is one at home or just buy one in a car boot sale.

Chocolate Fondue

1 x 250g block plain chocolate
½ pint/300ml tub of double cream
2 tablespoons brandy or rum

To dip
pineapple, strawberries, grapes, apples, bananas, marshamallows

Heat the chocolate gently on the cooker and add the cream. Stir frequently until it is quite warm, (just try it), then add the alcohol and heat a little more. Pour into the fondue pot and then place over the burner. Keep the burner low. Cut the larger fruit into bite-size chunks. Dip the fruits or marshmallows into the chocolate using the fondue forks.

Cheese Fondue

1 clove of garlic
1½ mugs dry white wine
3 mugs grated mild cheddar cheese
2 mugs grated Gruyere (Swiss) cheese
2 mugs grated Mozzarella cheese
1 tablespoon cornflour
pepper

1. Grate the cheeses.
2. Bruise the garlic and wipe it around the fondue pot. Discard the garlic.
3. Pour the wine into the pot and heat gently on the cooker. Gradually add the cheeses, stirring constantly. Stir until all the cheese has melted. Season with pepper
4. Mix the cornflour with a little water to make a paste and add to the cheese mixture, stirring well. The fondue should thicken. Transfer the pot to the fondue burner, keeping the heat low.

Dips for cheese fondue

French bread cut into bite-size chunks, apples, grapes

Sample Menu and Shopping Lists

These menus and shopping lists assume that you have time to cook 3 or 4 times during the week and eat sandwiches and fruit for lunch each day and cereal or toast for breakfast.

Sample Weekly Menu 1

Monday	Cook Quick Shepherds Pie
Tuesday	Eat rest of Shepherds Pie
Wednesday	Baked Potato and grated cheese
Thursday	Eggie Bread and Beans
Friday	Cook Chicken Risotto
Saturday	Eat the rest of the Chicken Risotto
Sunday	Cook Noodle Omelette and share it with a flatmate

Check Cupboards for:

Bisto or gravy granules
Rice
Curry paste
Chicken and beef stock cubes
Freeze dried chives
Salt and pepper

Shopping List

Small bag potatoes
1 yellow pepper
1 onion
Fruit for lunches
Few mushrooms

Bread
Cereal
Milk
½ doz eggs
Butter or marg.
Block of cheese

1 small tin sweetcorn
1 x 14 oz/400g tin baked beans
Fillings for sandwiches (see page 19)
Pack of small chicken fillets
500g pack mince

Sample Weekly Menu 2

Monday	Vegetable Soup, make enough for 2 days
Tuesday	Vegetable Soup
Wednesday	Baked Potato with Tuna and Mayo, use the rest of the tuna for sandwiches
Thursday	Chicken Casserole
Friday	Eat the rest of the Chicken Casserole
Saturday	Rosti and salad
Sunday	Beefy Mince & Pasta Bake, share with friend

Check Cupboards for:

Chicken stock cube
Flour
Worcestershire sauce
Mixed herbs
Rice
Pasta

Shopping List

1 small bag of potatoes
2 carrots
3 onions
Garlic
Celery, use for soup and sandwiches
Fruit for lunches
Salad
Ham

Bread
Milk
Cereal
Butter
Cheese
Eggs
Small pack frozen peas
Sandwich fillings

Small jar mayo
1 x 14 oz/400g tin chopped tomatoes
1 tin Campbell's condensed tomato soup
1 tin tuna
500g pack mince
4 chicken thighs

Shopping lists

Sample Weekly Menu 3

Monday	Spicy Risotto
Tuesday	Mince Hot Pot
Wednesday	Rest of Mince Hot Pot
Thursday	Roast Chicken and Potatoes
Friday	Use left over Chicken in omelette or with mayo and a baked potato
Saturday	Spaghetti Bolognese x 2
Sunday	Use left over Bolognese sauce, add curry paste and serve with rice

Check Cupboards for:

Rice
Pilau rice cubes/pilau seasoning
Freeze dried coriander
Curry paste
Stock cubes
Tomato puree
Mayo
Oil to cook with

Shopping List

10 mushrooms
Garlic
Medium bag of potatoes
4 onions
Fruit for lunches

Bread
Butter
Milk
Cereal
Sandwich fillings

2 x 14oz/400g tins of chopped tomatoes
1kg pack of mince
Small frozen chicken, approx. 1.5 kg, take out of the freezer the night before.

Sample Weekly Menu 4

Monday	Beans on toast with poached or fried egg on top
Tuesday	Tuna and Pasta Bake
Wednesday	Rest of Tuna and Pasta Bake
Thursday	Chicken and Sweetcorn Soup
Friday	Jacket Potato with cheese
Saturday	Pasta with Cheesy Sauce and Ham
Sunday	Potato Hash

Check Cupboards for:

Pasta
Chicken stock cube
Soy sauce
Freeze dried chives
Worcestershire sauce
Flour

Shopping List

2 onions
1 carrot
Few green beans
Bunch of spring onions
Fruit for lunches
Small bag of potatoes
2 mushrooms

Milk
Cereal
Butter
Eggs
Bread
Cheese
Sandwich fillings

1 tin Campbell's condensed mushroom soup
1 x 14 oz/400g tin baked beans
1 tin tuna
Small tin of sweetcorn
2 small chicken fillets
Ham
Tofu or tin of corned beef

Shopping lists

Sample Weekly Menu 5

Monday	Italian Soup
Tuesday	Scrambled egg on toast
Wednesday	Spaghetti Bolognese, make enough Bolognese sauce for 2 days
Thursday	Use rest of Bolognese Sauce, add chilli powder and serve with baked potato
Friday	Pasta with Tomato Sauce
Saturday	Chicken Curry
Sunday	Roast Potatoes and Sausages

Check Cupboards for:

Garlic
Chicken stock cube
Freeze dried basil
Tomato puree
Spaghetti
Chilli powder
Pasta
Oil for cooking
Curry paste

Shopping List

Small bag of potatoes
4 onions
7 mushrooms
I red pepper
I carrot
Celery, eat the excess with lunches
Packet of small macaroni
Fruit for lunches
Sandwich fillings

Milk
Bread
Cereal
Eggs
Butter
Small natural yoghurt
I x 14 oz/400g tin baked beans

I x 7 oz/200g tin of chopped tomatoes
2 x 14 oz/400g tins tomatoes
Frozen spinach
I chicken breast or 2 small fillets
I x 500g pack of mince
Ham for Friday and sandwiches

Sample Weekly Menu 6

Monday	Lancashire Hot Pot
Tuesday	Rest of Lancashire Hot Pot
Wednesday	Omelette with crispy bacon and tomatoes
Thursday	Mulligatawny Soup
Friday	Rest of Mulligatawny Soup
Saturday	Chicken and Nut Salad
Sunday	Potato Wedges and Sausages

Check Cupboards for:

Oil to cook with
Curry paste
Chicken stock cube
Rice
Garlic
Mayo
Freeze dried chives

Shopping List

3 onions
I carrot
Celery
Lettuce
½ Cucumber
I apple
Fresh tomatoes
Small bag of potatoes
Fruit for lunches

Milk
Bread
Cereal
Butter
Eggs
Cheese
Small carton of Creme Frais

Sausages
500g pack of cubed lamb/lamb mince
Small pack of bacon
4 small chicken breast fillets or 3 chicken breasts
Small packet of walnuts or pecans
Small packet of raisins
Sandwich fillings

Shopping lists

Index

V = Vegetarian   VO = Vegetarian option

V = vegetarian   VO = vegetarian option in the recipe

I studied Textile Design at Loughborough College of Art and Design from 1990 – 1994. Since then I have worked as a freelance designer. I have been married to Ron for 26 years, and our sons Ben and Tim have both graduated.

I started to cook cakes when I was 5 years old; by the time I was 12 my sister, Hilary, and I could cook a Sunday lunch! We would still have to do the washing up afterwards though! I have always loved cooking, especially for others, and there is nothing I like more than a house full of people to feed.

Many of the simple recipes in this book are things I first learned to cook but with a bit of a twist to make them more modern. I am pleased with the feedback I have had from students regarding the first edition of the book and hope that this second, improved, edition provides even more encouragement to students to enjoy cooking and have a healthier diet.